Women of Achievement

Jane Addams

Women of Achievement

Abigail Adams

Jane Addams

Susan B. Anthony

Tyra Banks

Clara Barton

Nellie Bly

Julia Child

Hillary Rodham
Clinton

Marie Curie

Ellen DeGeneres

Diana, Princess
of Wales

Amelia Earhart

Tina Fey

Ruth Bader Ginsburg

Joan of Arc

Angelina Jolie

Helen Keller

Madonna

Michelle Obama

Sandra Day O'Connor

Georgia O'Keeffe

Nancy Pelosi

Rachael Ray

Anita Roddick

Eleanor Roosevelt

Martha Stewart

Barbara Walters

Venus and Serena
Williams

Women of Achievement

Jane Addams

HUMANITARIAN

Louise Chipley Slavicek

CHELSEA HOUSE
An Infobase Learning Company

JANE ADDAMS

Chelsea House
An imprint of Infobase Learning
132 West 31st Street
New York, NY 10001

Library of Congress Cataloging-in-Publication Data
Slavicek, Louise Chipley, 1956–
  Jane Addams : humanitarian / by Louise Chipley Slavicek.
    p. cm. — (Women of achievement)
  Includes bibliographical references and index.
  ISBN 978-1-60413-907-5 (hardcover)
  1. Addams, Jane, 1860–1935—Juvenile literature. 2. Women social reformers—United States—Biography—Juvenile literature. 3. Social workers—United States—Biography—Juvenile literature. 4. Hull House (Chicago, Ill.)—Juvenile literature. I. Title. II. Series.

  HV28.A35S53 2011
  361.92—dc22
  [B]

                                    2011000038

Chelsea House books are available at special discounts when purchased in bulk quantities for businesses, associations, institutions, or sales promotions. Please call our Special Sales Department in New York at (212) 967-8800 or (800) 322-8755.

You can find Chelsea House on the World Wide Web
at http://www.infobaselearning.com.

Text design by Erik Lindstrom
Cover design by Ben Peterson and Alicia Post
Composition by EJB Publishing Services
Cover printed by Yurchak Printing, Landisville, Pa.
Book printed and bound by Yurchak Printing, Landisville, Pa.
Date printed: August 2011
Printed in the United States of America

10 9 8 7 6 5 4 3 2 1

This book is printed on acid-free paper.

All links and Web addresses were checked and verified to be correct at the time of publication. Because of the dynamic nature of the Web, some addresses and links may have changed since publication and may no longer be valid.

CONTENTS

"The Highest Possibilities of the Human Spirit"

Jane Addams would always remember her first Christmas as director of Hull House, the settlement house she had founded in Chicago's crowded and squalid Nineteenth Ward just three months earlier with her friend, schoolteacher Ellen Gates Starr. Starr and Addams, the college-educated daughter of a prosperous Illinois businessman and lawmaker, had moved into the decaying mansion once owned by Chicago real estate tycoon Charles Hull in September 1889. Influenced by the budding settlement movement in London's destitute East End, the two pioneering social workers had resolved to "settle" or live among Chicago's most impoverished residents. Using the rambling Hull home as their base, the women intended to provide educational and cultural uplift to the Nineteenth Ward's poor immigrant residents through a wide range of free classes, lectures, and clubs. It did not take long, however, for Addams to realize that her new neighbors needed a great deal more than cultural and intellectual uplift from her and Hull House's growing staff of middle- and upper-class volunteers. As Addams would later reveal in her best-selling autobiography, *Twenty Years at Hull-House*, her education regarding the true nature of her downtrodden neighbors' plight began at the first of the settlement house's annual Christmas parties.

At the party, held shortly before Christmas Day 1889, Addams and Starr planned to hand out candy to all of the boys and girls who attended. They figured that candy would be a welcome luxury for children whose parents struggled to provide them with even the most basic necessities of life. Addams and Starr were much surprised, therefore, when a group of little girls who arrived at the party together refused to accept the sugary treats. The girls explained that they could not bear the sight of candy.

All were employed by a local candy manufacturer, and ever since the Christmas rush season had begun six weeks before, their boss had made them toil "from seven in the morning until nine at night" at the factory every day except Sunday. Quitting was not an option for the children. The girls' families depended on their wages, even though their hourly pay was disgracefully low. "The sharp consciousness of stern economic conditions was thus thrust upon us in the midst of the season of good will," Addams wrote in *Twenty Years at Hull-House*.[1] Soon after this eye-opening incident, Addams received another shock when three young boys in the neighborhood were seriously hurt while operating machinery at a nearby factory. After one boy died from his injuries, Addams tried to shame the factory owner into doing something about his plant's dangerous working conditions. As she noted in *Twenty Years*, however, the factory

Jane Addams, shown here in 1890, cofounded Hull House the year before to provide educational and cultural opportunities to the impoverished immigrant residents of Chicago's Nineteenth Ward. She soon discovered, however, that her neighbors had more pressing economic needs.

owner was so indifferent to the well-being of his employees, child and adult, that he could not even be bothered to install inexpensive safety guards on his machines.

Addams was forever changed by her crash course in the grim realities of industrial working conditions in Gilded Age America during her first winter at Hull House. By the early 1890s, encouraged by several reform-minded Hull House colleagues, Addams had expanded her humanitarian efforts on behalf of the urban poor to include fighting for protective legislation for workers, including statutes prohibiting factories from hiring children under the age of 15 and mandating eight-hour workdays and safer work environments. Throughout the rest of her life, Addams would continue to campaign for local and national laws and policies that addressed the social and economic injustices she believed to be at the root of urban poverty and to champion the country's underserved and oppressed, including women, African Americans, and immigrants. During the last two decades of her life, she was also a tireless advocate for international peace, winning the Nobel Peace Prize for her efforts in 1931.

Following Jane Addams's death in 1935 at age 74, tributes to America's most famous and admired female humanitarian poured into Hull House from around the nation and the globe. One of the most moving and eloquent eulogies to her was written by the newspaper commentator Walter Lippmann. He wrote of Addams:

> She had compassion without condescension. She had pity without retreat into vulgarity. She had infinite sympathy for common things without forgetfulness of those that are uncommon. That, I think, is why those who have known her say that she was not only good, but great. For this blend of sympathy with distinction, of common humanity with a noble

style is recognizable by those who have eyes to see it as the occasional but authentic issue of the mystic promise of the American democracy. It is the quality which reached its highest expression in Lincoln, when, out of the rudeness of his background and amidst the turmoil of his times, he spoke in accents so pure that his words ring true enduringly. This is the ultimate vindication of the democratic faith, not that men can be brought to a common level, but that without pomp or pride or power or privilege, every man might and some men will achieve again and again the highest possibilities of the human spirit.[2]

Her Father's Daughter

Jane Addams was born on September 6, 1860, near the farming village of Cedarville, Illinois, just south of the Wisconsin border. Jane was the eighth child of Sarah Weber Addams, a housewife, and John Huy Addams, a well-off farmer and mill owner and, for the previous six years, an Illinois state senator. Shortly after marrying in their home state of Pennsylvania in 1844, Sarah and John headed west to the largely unsettled prairies of northern Illinois in search of greater economic opportunities. Their first child, Mary, was born one year later, followed by Martha in 1850, John Weber in 1852, and Alice in 1853. Three other children—two boys and a girl—died as babies before Jane arrived, when John was 37 and Sarah was 42 years old.

JANE'S MOTHER: SARAH WEBER ADDAMS

In common with the lives of most American women of her era, Sarah Addams's life revolved around caring for her family and home. Owing in large measure to a profitable investment they made in a local railroad company, the Addamses had quickly prospered after arriving in Illinois with just enough cash to purchase a mill and several hundred acres of farmland. Consequently, they were among the fortunate few in Cedarville who could afford to employ house servants. Yet, even with the assistance of a nursemaid, a laundress, and two hired girls, a seemingly endless list of chores filled Sarah's days. Responsible for planning and helping prepare meals for the up to two-dozen farmhands and mill workers employed by her husband at any given time, she also toiled side by side with her servants making soap, candles, quilts, and rugs; sewing and mending clothing; baking bread; and preserving vegetables and fruits.

Known for her quiet, serene manner, Sarah Addams nonetheless possessed a great deal of inner confidence and determination. John was often away from home on business or attending sessions of the Illinois legislature in Springfield, nearly 200 miles (322 kilometers) away. While he was gone, Sarah single-handedly ran the family farm, sawmill, and gristmill, where neighbors brought their grain to be ground into flour, in addition to managing her large household.

On an icy January day in 1863, when Jane was not quite 2½, Sarah suffered a terrible accident. Sarah was always ready to aid a community member in need. Thus, although she was seven months pregnant herself, Sarah had generously volunteered to assist a neighbor who was having a difficult labor and childbirth. On her way home from the neighbor's house, Sarah slipped and fell on the hard, frozen ground. Within a week of the accident, she and her infant had both died. Many years later, Jane could still vividly recall pounding on her dying mother's bedroom door with her fists, begging to be allowed to see her. Through her sobs, Jane was sure she heard Sarah cry out, "Let her in, she is only a baby herself." That haunting image was Jane Addams's only memory of her mother.[1]

JANE AND HER FATHER

After her mother's death, Jane clung to her two oldest sisters, 17-year-old Mary, who assumed the household's day-to-day management, and 13-year-old Martha. The family member Jane yearned to be closest to, however, was her serious and hardworking father. In her autobiography, *Twenty Years at Hull-House*, published in 1910, Jane described John Addams as "the dominant influence" of her childhood and the object "of my supreme affection." On him, Jane wrote, she centered "all that careful imitation which a little girl ordinarily gives to her mother's ways and habits."[2]

Jane was determined to be as much like her beloved parent as possible. To that end, she put in long days at the family gristmill, trying to give herself the flattened "miller's thumb" that John Addams had acquired from repeatedly pressing his thumb against a millstone when he was a young miller's apprentice in Pennsylvania. In her autobiography, Jane recalled spending countless hours "rubbing between my thumb and fingers the ground wheat as it fell from between the millstones" in hopes of making her hands resemble those of her hero's.[3] She also forced herself to rise at 3:00 A.M. with her father, who had developed the habit of waking before dawn as a teenaged apprentice. Jane imagined her father, an avid, lifelong reader, eventually making his way through every book in the village library during his early morning turns at the Pennsylvania mill where he learned his trade. Inspired by his example, Jane resolved to put her long mornings to good use by reading every volume in her father's vast book collection, which took up nearly

DID YOU KNOW?

Aside from her father, the person Jane Addams admired most during her childhood was Abraham Lincoln. Probably not coincidentally, Lincoln was also John Addams's hero. Like Lincoln, John Addams detested slavery and in 1854 joined the newly created Republican Party, which opposed the extension of slavery into the Western territories. That same year, Addams was elected to the Illinois State Senate. While he was in Springfield attending legislative sessions, Addams befriended Lincoln, who was a prominent lawyer in the state capital before his election to the presidency in November 1860.

Over the years, Addams and Lincoln exchanged a number of letters, most of them about legislative matters of concern to Lincoln. Jane fondly remembered her father reading aloud to her from Lincoln's letters, which invariably opened with the humorous salutation: "My dear Double-dee'd Addams." She also recalled her father displaying two pictures of Lincoln in prominent spots in his study and a third picture of the president with his young son, Tad, in the upstairs parlor. When news of Lincoln's assassination in April 1865 reached Cedarville, four-and-a-half-year-old Jane was shocked to

One of Jane Addams's childhood heroes was President Abraham Lincoln. While serving as a state senator in Springfield, Illinois, Addams's father became friends with Lincoln, and the two often exchanged letters. John Addams would read those letters to his daughter.

(continues)

(continued)

see her normally reserved father weeping. "The greatest man in the world has just died," he explained to her. "For one or all of these reasons I always tend to associate Lincoln with the tenderest thoughts of my father," she wrote in her autobiography nearly a half century later.*

---

* Jane Addams, *Twenty Years at Hull-House*. New York: Macmillan, 1910, p. 32.

the entire second-floor parlor of the Addamses' big, gray brick house. John Addams was so delighted by Jane's ambitious plan that he offered to pay her to finish those books he believed to be most important to her intellectual and moral development. Jane later recalled her father giving her a nickel for each volume she read by the Greek historian and essayist Plutarch and a dollar for completing American author Washington Irving's four-volume biography of George Washington.

When she was very young, Jane contracted tuberculosis of the spine. As a result, she was left with a slightly curved back, which caused her to walk with her toes pointed inward, in a pigeon-toed manner. By all accounts, Jane was an exceptionally pretty child with large, deep-set gray eyes and fine, reddish-brown hair. For a time, however, she was convinced that her "crooked" back and awkward way of walking made her an "ugly duckling" and a source of secret embarrassment to her successful and dignified father. Consequently, when Jane and John Addams were out in public and strangers were around, she tried to keep her distance from her father, in hopes that no one would guess she was his daughter. Jane was finally cured of her painful insecurities regarding how her appearance reflected on her parent during a visit to the neighboring city of Freeport. To her horror, she unexpectedly ran into her father right in the middle of the busiest street in town. In her autobiography, Jane described what happened next:

> With a playful touch of exaggeration, he lifted his high and shining silk hat and made me an imposing bow. This distinguished public recognition, this totally unnecessary identification among a mass of "strange people" who couldn't possibly know unless he himself made the sign, suddenly filled me with a sense of the absurdity of the entire feeling.[4]

Her father's chivalrous public acknowledgment of her was a transforming moment for Jane. From then on, she felt confident that her physical flaw had in no way diminished her in the eyes of her father, who was as proud of his youngest as he was of his four straight-backed children.

JANE'S AWAKENING CONSCIENCE

In her quest to be as much like her beloved father as possible, Jane struggled to live up to his high moral standards. Addams's sense of duty and honesty were legendary. A Chicago political reporter once commented that Senator Addams's reputation for integrity was so well known that no one would even think to offer a bribe to him. Her father, Jane recalled as an adult, "was the uncompromising enemy of wrong and of wrong doing."[5] If she ever told a lie to her father, no matter how small, Jane would feel so guilty that she could not sleep until she had confessed her misdeed to him. After groping her way downstairs in the dark, she recalled: "I would finally reach my father's bedside perfectly breathless and having panted out the history of my sin,

IN HER OWN WORDS

In *Twenty Years at Hull-House,* Jane Addams described a childhood incident involving her serious-minded father and a pretty new cloak of which she was very proud.

> Although I constantly confided my sins and perplexities to my father, there are only a few occasions on which I remember having received direct advice or admonition. . . . I can remember an admonition on one occasion, however, when, as a little girl of eight years, arrayed in a new cloak, gorgeous beyond anything I had ever worn before, I stood before my father for his approval. I was much chagrined by his remark that it was a very pretty cloak—in fact so much prettier than any cloak the other little girls in the Sunday School had, that he would advise me to wear my old cloak, which would keep me quite as warm, with the added advantage of not making the other little girls feel badly. I complied with the request but I fear without inner consent, and I certainly was quite without the joy of self-sacrifice as I walked soberly through the village street by the side of my counselor. My mind was busy, however, with the old question eternally suggested by the inequalities of the human lot. Only as we neared the church door did I venture to ask what could be done about it, receiving the reply that it might never be righted so far as clothes went, but that people might be equal in things that mattered much more than clothes, the affairs of education and religion, for instance, which we attended to when we went to school and church, and that it was very stupid to wear the sort of clothes that made it harder to have equality even there.*

---

* Jane Addams, *Twenty Years at Hull-House.* New York: Macmillan, 1910, pp. 13–14.

invariably received the same assurance that if he 'had a little girl who told lies,' he was very glad that she 'felt too bad to go to sleep afterward.' "[6]

In addition to his strict personal integrity, John Addams's humanitarian spirit and civic conscience also made a big impression on Jane. Devoutly religious, Addams was convinced that Christians had a sacred duty to lessen human suffering and create a more just and caring society. To that end, he donated generously to a host of charitable causes and was actively involved in promoting public education and more humane treatment for the mentally ill. (Although some of Jane's biographers have described him as a Quaker, John Addams did not belong to the Quaker or any other religious denomination. The family regularly attended the Cedarville Presbyterian Church and several other Protestant churches in the area during Jane's childhood but never officially joined any of them.)

Ever her father's child, even as a small girl, "the injustices of the world troubled her deeply," Jane's biographer Gioia Diliberto writes.[7] One day, when Jane was seven, she and her father drove through a destitute section of Freeport that she had never seen before. Jane was shocked by how run-down and crowded together the houses were. When she indignantly asked her father why anyone would want to live "in such horrid little houses so close together," he replied that the slum's impoverished inhabitants could afford nothing better. "After receiving his explanation," Jane recalled in *Twenty Years at Hull-House*, "I declared with much firmness when I grew up I should, of course, have a large house, but it would not be built among the other large houses, but right in the midst of horrid little houses like these."[8]

Around the same time as the Freeport episode, Jane began to have a recurring nightmare. In the dream, everyone in the world was dead, except for herself. Suddenly, she was struck by the overpowering conviction that human civilization could only be revived if she reinvented the wheel. Night after night, she dreamed that she stood in a deserted blacksmith shop, "darkly pondering" how to go about constructing a wheel.[9] The nightmare seemed so real to Jane that, on the day after she had the dream, she would often visit the village blacksmith shop to grill its mystified owner about how to forge molten iron into a wagon wheel.

A NEW STEPMOTHER

In 1868, five years after Sarah's death, John Addams remarried. His new wife was Anna Haldeman, an attractive and high-strung widow and mother of two from Freeport. Although she had received little formal education, compared with most residents of Cedarville, Anna was unusually well read and cultured. An accomplished pianist and guitarist, she loved art and literature as well as music. Anna was also a bit of a snob. She enjoyed throwing elegant dinner parties for her well-off Freeport friends and driving around Cedarville in a showy carriage that she had persuaded her reluctant husband to purchase. "Compared with Sarah Addams's even, homey nature, Anna's manner was haughty," author Diliberto writes. "The neighbors thought she was 'putting on airs.'"[10]

Most people who knew Anna agreed that she could be short-tempered and conceited at times. Yet, despite her shortcomings, she was an attentive stepmother, particularly to her youngest stepchild, Jane. Anna's especially close relationship with Jane probably had a great deal to do with the fact that, within three years of her and John's wedding, Jane was the only Addams child still living at home. Tragically, Martha had died of typhoid fever in 1866, when she was just 16. By late 1871, Alice was a boarding student at Rockford Female Seminary, about 30 miles (48 kilometers) away in Rockford, Illinois; John Weber was working

In 1868, John Addams married Anna Haldeman, a widow from nearby Freeport, Illinois. Anna had a son, George, who was just six months younger than Jane Addams. For the first time, young Jane had a playmate her own age, and the two could often be found exploring the countryside by their home. This portrait from 1876 shows Jane at age 16, with her stepmother and George.

and living on his own; and Mary had wed John Linn, a local Presbyterian minister.

According to Jane's biographer Allen F. Davis, although Jane "was somewhat aghast at her stepmother's outbursts of temper," soon "a real bond of affection developed between her and her stepmother. Jane referred to her very naturally as 'Ma,' and Anna treated the quiet, retiring child as one of her own."[11] Anna encouraged Jane, who had previously shied away from all athletic activities, to take up horseback riding to help strengthen her back. To Jane's delight, Anna also introduced her to the world of fiction, which John Addams had always looked down on as frivolous. The novels of the English writer Charles Dickens and the classic young person's novel, *Little Women* by Louisa May Alcott, quickly became Jane's favorite books. For Jane, however, the greatest benefit of her father's marriage to the Widow Haldeman was that it brought Anna's young son, George, into the Addams household.

JANE AND GEORGE

When John Addams wed Anna Haldeman in the autumn of 1868, Harry, the eldest of Anna's two children by her first husband, was 20 years old and living independently. (Harry, who married Jane's sister, Alice, in 1875, eventually became a physician and businessman). George, Anna's much younger second son, was seven-and-a-half. He and Jane, who had just turned eight when the Addams and Haldeman families merged, quickly became inseparable playmates and best friends. "For the first time Jane had someone with whom to have adventures, concoct complicated imaginary games, and share confessions," author Louise Knight writes.[12] "Until George came, a 'sense of solitude' had been too much with her," Jane's nephew, James Weber Linn, observes in his *Jane Addams: A Biography*. "George's presence drove it away."[13]

All aspects of science and the natural world fascinated George, who passed this enthusiasm on to his stepsister. During their summer vacations and on weekends, Jane and George spent countless hours exploring the rolling countryside near the Addams home. They climbed limestone cliffs in search of owl's nests, combed forests and fields for unusual plant specimens, and explored mysterious caves by candlelight. They also hunted snakes and, inspired by their

JANE AND THE PHRENOLOGIST

In July 1876, when she was not quite 16, Jane was evaluated by John Capen, a well-known Philadelphia phrenologist, while she and her family were in the City of Brotherly Love to attend the first world's fair held in the United States. At the time, phrenology, which claimed to reveal a person's natural character, strengths, and weaknesses through a close examination of the size and shape of his or her skull, was all the rage in America.

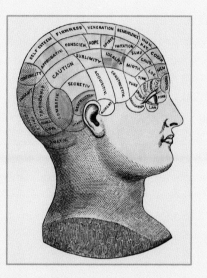

Phrenology, a popular pseudo-science in the late 1800s, purported to reveal a person's characteristics through the size and shape of his or her head. In 1876, while attending the world's fair in Philadelphia, Jane Addams visited a well-known phrenologist. This phrenology model shows the locations of the "various organs of the mind" on the human head.

Addams must have been taken by Capen's interpretation of her natural personality traits, because she kept the report he prepared on her in 1876 for the rest of her life. After Addams's death in 1935, her nephew discovered the document among her personal papers. According to Capen's supposedly "scientific" evaluation of her cranium, Addams was "inclined to be serious and earnest. . . . If she thinks a thing is true, she thinks

(continues)

(continued)
it with all her might." Her main weakness, the phrenologist declared, was that she suffered from a "lack of confidence in herself."* But, he concluded, Addams was also "steady and persevering, sticking to a thing when the majority give it up. She will come out near the head at last."**

---

* Quoted in Louise W. Knight, *Citizen: Jane Addams and the Struggle for Democracy.* Chicago: University of Chicago Press, p. 75.
** Gioia Diliberto, *A Useful Woman: The Early Life of Jane Addams.* New York: Scribner, 1999, p. 57.

classroom studies of ancient civilizations, ritually sacrificed the reptiles to imaginary deities on a makeshift altar by a favorite stream.

George never coddled Jane either because she had a malformed spine or because she was a female at a time when girls, at least those from the middle or upper classes, were generally thought of as more fragile than males. By expecting Jane to take an active role in all of his expeditions and adventures, no matter how strenuous, risky, or "unladylike," George "made her feel she was the equal of any boy," author Barbara Garland Polikoff observes.[14] Jane more than lived up to her stepbrother's expectations for her when George made the mistake of trying to capture a muskrat he had spotted in the creek with his bare hands. The muskrat clamped its sharp teeth into George's hand and refused to let go until, deciding there was no other way to free her playmate, Jane put her squeamishness aside and cut the animal's head off with a penknife.

By the time Jane and George were in their mid-teens, George had decided to pursue his love of science by majoring in biology at all-male Beloit College in Wisconsin and then enrolling in medical school after graduation. Encouraged by her stepbrother, Jane decided that she, too, would study for a college degree and continue on to medical school, even though only a tiny number of American women graduated from college in the late 1800s, and even fewer earned medical degrees. After finishing medical school, she planned to work with society's most downtrodden, like the impoverished inhabitants of the crowded hovels that had so shocked her when she first saw Freeport's slums with her father. Yet, though John Addams had always encouraged his daughter to develop her natural intellectual abilities and her social conscience, Jane's ambitious and unconventional educational and career goals would place her in direct conflict with her adored father for the first time in her life.

An Educated Woman

In later years, Jane Addams fondly remembered her father encouraging her to think for herself and trust her own judgment during her growing-up years. In an essay published in 1912, she recalled John Addams's reaction after she "bungled" the arrangements for a big family celebration when she was in her teens and he and Anna were out of town. In apologizing for the fiasco, Jane told him she had just been trying to handle the arrangements as she thought he would have. "You fell into the easy mistake of substituting loyalty and dependence on another's judgment for the best use of your own faculties," John admonished his daughter. "You will do much better if you look the situation fairly in the face with the best light you have."[1]

"I WAS . . . RESENTFUL"

Addams apparently forgot his earlier advice to Jane about trusting her own judgment when, during her senior year in high school, she decided she wanted to earn a bachelor's degree from prestigious Smith College in Northampton, Massachusetts. Founded in 1871, Smith was one of the first all-female colleges in the United States.

"I was very ambitious to go to Smith," Jane recalled in *Twenty Years at Hull-House*.[2] Jane had set her sights on the Massachusetts institution because, of the handful of American women's schools that offered bachelor's degrees in the 1870s, "more than the others, Smith tried to maintain the same standards as the best men's colleges," Allen Davis writes.[3] Smith's science curriculum was particularly rigorous, a definite advantage for Jane should she attend medical school after completing her undergraduate studies. To Jane's great disappointment, however, John Addams refused to send her to Smith. Instead, he insisted she enroll at the same school her three older sisters had attended—nearby Rockford Female Seminary, which did not award Bachelor's of Art or Science degrees. (John Addams sent his only surviving son, John Weber, to the University of Michigan in 1868. John Weber, who was plagued by physical and mental illnesses for much of his adult life, dropped out of college before the end of his freshmen year, however.)

Probably out of loyalty to her father, Jane barely mentioned her disagreement with him about her education in her memoirs or other published writings. Shortly before her death at age 74, however, Addams confessed to her nephew James Weber Linn that, as she headed off to Rockford Seminary in 1877, instead of the more academically challenging eastern college that had been her first choice, "I was . . . resentful, I suppose you might call it." Jane desperately wanted a college degree, Linn observes in his biography of her: "However, John Addams's word was law with his daughter, and she made no fuss about the matter."[4] Writes Gioia Diliberto:

> The college choice illustrated a conflict that troubled [Jane] for years; on the one hand, she wanted to believe she could accomplish anything she set her mind to do; on the other, she felt pressured by "family claims," by demands she conform to her parents' wishes.[5]

WOMEN AND HIGHER EDUCATION IN THE LATE 1800s

John Addams's unwillingness to send his youngest daughter to a first-rank college such as Smith was unsurprising, given prevailing attitudes toward women and higher education in the late nineteenth century. During the mid-1870s, less than one percent of college-aged women in the United States were enrolled at institutions that awarded bachelor's degrees. A majority of the relatively small number of women who continued their education beyond high school attended all-female academies or "seminaries," like Rockford Female Seminary, which offered less difficult and varied academic coursework than most colleges and universities, particularly in the areas of science and mathematics. The tiny female elite who enrolled in institutions that granted bachelor's degrees either attended forward-looking, coeducational schools such as Cornell or Oberlin or one of a handful of women's colleges founded during the 1860s and 1870s, the most notable being Vassar in New York and Smith and Wellesley in Massachusetts.

Like other late-nineteenth-century American parents who were able and willing to provide their daughters with a postsecondary education but drew the line at sending them to a full-fledged college, John and Anna Addams held

TERRIBLE RESULT OF THE HIGHER EDUCATION OF WOMEN!

Miss Hypatia Jones, Spinster of Arts (on her way to Refreshment), informs Profess: Parallax, F.R.S., that "Young Men do very well to Look at, or to Dance with, or even to Marry, and all that kind of Thing!" but that "as to enjoying any Ratio: .l. .on with any Man under Fifty, that is completely out of the Question!"

In the late nineteenth century, the prevailing sentiment was that higher education was a wasteful luxury for women. It was thought that women belonged at home and that they were too frail for grueling college work. This illustration from 1874 from *Punch* depicts a more frivolous reason for opposition, as the young women students go into dinner on the arms of their professors while the young men languish against the wall.

traditional ideas regarding the proper role of women in society. Throughout the 1800s, it was generally assumed that women belonged at home, caring for their husbands and children, and most professional careers were closed to them. Consequently, American parents typically viewed a college degree as a wasteful luxury for their female children. Jane's quick mind and love of learning delighted John Addams, and he took pride in his ability to provide her with several years of study at a reputable female seminary followed by a year or two of travel abroad to further broaden her intellectual and cultural horizons. But he was uncomfortable with Jane's ambitious educational and professional goals. His chief aspiration for Jane, as for her older sisters, was that she should secure a marriage proposal from an educated and industrious man—just the kind of man likely to be drawn to an accomplished woman like herself—and raise a family.

Jane's stepmother was in complete agreement with her husband regarding a woman's highest calling in life. In a letter Anna wrote to John shortly after their marriage, she ridiculed the women's rights movement, which had first developed in the United States during the 1840s and demanded greater legal rights and career opportunities for women. Feminist leaders like Susan B. Anthony, she scoffed, would have women "do away with *baby* and *cradle* and ape instead a *statesmanship* or *professorship*."[6]

In addition to his and Anna's traditional attitudes toward the proper place of women in society, another factor behind John Addams's reluctance to send Jane to Smith College may have been concerns regarding her health. During the late nineteenth century, many people believed that intensive intellectual training was injurious to young women. Supposedly, vigorous and prolonged mental activity was too taxing for their "delicate" bodies and minds. In his pamphlet of 1867, "Women's Rights," popular author John Todd asked: "Must we crowd education upon our daughters, and for the sake of having them 'intellectual,' make them puny, nervous, and their whole earthly existence a struggle between life and death?"[7] Six years later, such popular prejudices regarding higher education for women received "scientific" support from Dr. Edward Clarke, a Harvard Medical School professor. His best-selling book, *Sex in Education or a Fair Chance for the Girls*, claimed that young women lacked the physical and mental resilience to handle grueling class schedules and late-night study sessions. Their anatomy, particularly their reproductive and nervous systems, was too frail for the demands of college life, Clarke insisted. Female college students, he warned dramatically, placed themselves at risk of infertility, insanity, and even death.

ANNA SILL AND THE ROCKFORD FEMALE SEMINARY

When 17-year-old Jane Addams began her studies at Rockford in September 1877, the school was just over a quarter of a century old. Rockford Female Seminary was chartered in 1847 by Congregational and Presbyterian leaders to provide religious, cultural, and domestic instruction to young women in Illinois and Wisconsin. But the seminary did not actually open its doors until 1851, after its first principal, 35-year-old Anna Peck Sill, raised $5,000 from the Rockford community to help build and staff the school.

From the beginning, Sill's strong Christian faith and unyielding moral principles molded the seminary's fundamental mission and character. When Jane enrolled at Rockford 26 years after Sill was first appointed its director, the indomitable 61-year-old was as vitally involved in every aspect of the seminary's academic, religious, and disciplinary practices as she had ever been. Sill's fondest hope was that her students would go on to serve God as Protestant missionaries after graduation. Consequently, she made sure that evangelical Protestantism took a central place in the school's routines and curriculum. (Evangelical Protestantism emphasizes personal conversion experiences and evangelism—the spreading of Christianity through preaching or missionary work—at home and abroad.) The "chief end of Woman's education is . . . to teach the great Christian lesson, that the true end of life is not to acquire the most good, whether of happiness or knowledge," Miss

Sill declared, "but to give oneself fully and worthily for the good of others."[8]

Although many female seminaries and academies allowed their students to board with local families, Sill required all Rockford students to live in the seminary's dormitories and forbade them to leave campus for any reason without her permission. The girls' highly structured days began at 5:00 A.M., when they were awakened by the loud clanging of the chapel bell. After dumping the ashes from

DID YOU KNOW?

Despite his conservative views regarding women and higher education, Jane Addams's father was a firm supporter of giving American women the right to vote, a privilege they finally won in 1920 with the ratification of the Nineteenth Amendment. After hearing suffragist Mary Livermore speak before the Illinois legislature in Springfield in February 1869, John Addams had become convinced that voting rights should be extended to all women along with African-American males, as the Fifteenth Amendment to the Constitution, then being debated in Congress, proposed. In a letter to his wife, Anna, on

Despite John Addams's opposition to Jane's education and career goals, he did believe that women should have the right to vote. The words of Mary Livermore (above), who spoke before the Illinois legislature in 1869, helped to sway John Addams's position on the issue.

the wood-burning stoves that heated their rooms and per-forming various chores in the school kitchen, the students filed into the communal dining room for breakfast at 7:00 sharp. A teacher presided over every table, and students were not allowed to sit down until the principal gave the signal. Morning chapel inevitably followed, with Miss Sill delivering a sermon on the day's Bible passage, which the girls were expected to recite from memory. Attendance at Sunday morning church services was also mandatory,

February 20, 1869, written shortly after attending Livermore's talk, John praised the 48-year-old women's rights activist for her "well-organized, . . . strong and convincing arguments."*

Anna Addams was as skeptical of women's suffrage as she was of the women's rights movement generally, and Jane's two oldest siblings, Mary and John Weber, were also opposed to granting women the vote. There is no record of what Jane herself thought of women's suffrage during her childhood. When Addams was in her seventies, however, she revealed to her nephew, James Weber Linn, that one of the women she most admired was suffragist Lucy Stone, who had been especially active during the 1870s, when Jane was in her teens. Although there is no record that Stone spoke in Cedarville or anywhere else in northern Illinois during the 1870s, Jane could easily have read her speeches on women's suffrage, since they were frequently reprinted in the *New York Tribune*, to which John Addams subscribed.

---

* Quoted in Louise W. Knight, *Citizen: Jane Addams and the Struggle for Democracy*. Chicago: University of Chicago Press, p. 63.

as were lengthy evening prayer meetings on the Sabbath. There were also more informal prayer meetings each weekday evening, between the girls' two required study periods. Once a month, Sill declared a school-wide fast day, during which students had to give up all food for 24 hours as a form of spiritual discipline. Each January, after the girls returned from Christmas break, the seminary suspended classes for a weeklong religious revival during which students who had not yet undergone a personal salvation experience were strongly encouraged to repent their sins and open their hearts to Christ.

Sill's influence on Rockford's academic program was almost as strong as her influence on its extracurricular routines. In addition to instruction in history, literature, government, science, Latin, German, and ancient Greek (the last so that students could read the Christian scriptures in their original language), Rockford women were required to take a variety of religious courses. Among them were "Evidences of Christianity," "Moral Philosophy," and several classes on the Hebrew and Christian scriptures (generally referred to by Christians as the Old and New Testaments).

"CLINGING TO INDIVIDUAL CONVICTION"

Jane had little choice but to comply with the required religious coursework and rituals, but inwardly she was uncomfortable with the seminary's evangelical bent. Although she had attended Sunday services with her family in Cedarville, following her father's lead, she had never formally joined a church. Her father had always emphasized living according to Christian moral principles, particularly charity and compassion toward others, over religious doctrine, and he encouraged her to be honest with herself about what she actually believed. For example, as a schoolgirl Jane had puzzled over the traditional Calvinist doctrine of predestination, which states that even before a person is born, God has foreordained whether he or she will enjoy eternal life. When Jane confessed her doubts regarding the harsh doctrine to her father, to her surprise, John Addams admitted that he had trouble accepting predestination as well. What was important, he said, was that she should never feel obliged to pretend that she understood predestination or any other religious tenet that perplexed her.

Jane's religious independence created problems for her with Miss Sill, who repeatedly pressured her to join a church and take a larger part in the school's annual revival. Although Jane stubbornly resisted the principal's demands, deep down, she "also worried about whether she

IN HER OWN WORDS

Once, during a class on moral philosophy taught by Anna Sill, Jane Addams dared to criticize the principal's pronunciation of the title of the famous Spanish novel, *Don Quixote*. Instead of giving it the more familiar Spanish pronunciation, as Jane did, Sill insisted on saying "Don Quix-ott." When the entire class backed up Jane by laughing at the principal's unusual pronunciation, Sill angrily canceled class for two days. At a mandatory chapel service later that morning, a defiant Jane wrote on the flyleaf of a classmate's hymnal:

> Life is a burden, bear it.
> Life's a duty, dare it.
> Life's a thorn crown? Wear it
>   And spurn to be a coward!*

---

* Quoted in James Weber Linn, *Jane Addams: A Biography.* 1935. Reprint. Urbana: University of Illinois Press, 2000, p. 48.

was doing the right thing," author Knight writes.[9] Writing nearly three decades later about her refusal to give in to Sill, Addams decided that, in the last analysis, her youthful rebellion against her pious headmistress had had a positive impact on her character development. With more than a hint of sarcasm, Addams declared that "this passive resistance of mine, this clinging to individual conviction," even in the face of the formidable Miss Sill's disapproval, was perhaps "the best moral training I received at Rockford."[10]

SETTLING IN AT ROCKFORD

Despite her discomfort with the school's strongly evangelical character and her disappointment at having to give up her dream of attending a first-rate women's college, Jane quickly settled into life at Rockford and made many new friends. The most important of them was Ellen Gates Starr, from the small town of Durand, Illinois.

Like Jane, Ellen loved ideas and learning. The two friends had long and passionate discussions regarding literature, art, and theology. Jane, who struggled to define her religious beliefs, could not help but envy Ellen's devout Christian faith and deeply spiritual nature. "You long for a beautiful faith," Jane once wrote to her friend.

> I only feel that I need religion in a practical sense, that if I fix myself with relations to God and the universe, & so be in perfect harmony with nature and Deity, I could use my faculties and energy so much better and could do almost anything. *Mine* is preeminently selfish and *yours* Ellen is reaching for higher things.[11]

To Jane's great disappointment, financial issues forced Ellen to withdraw from Rockford after just one year. Starr immediately went to work as a schoolteacher, first in a

As a student at Rockford Female Seminary, Jane Addams was uncomfortable with the school director's evangelical leanings. Still, she pursued a demanding course load, attracted many friends, and was elected president of the class of 1881.

small town near Durand and later at an elite girls' school in Chicago. Jane and Ellen kept in close touch by mail, however, and their friendship remained strong throughout Addams's four years at Rockford.

While Ellen was known for her outgoing personality, Jane was more reserved, like her father. Despite her natural reticence, however, the other girls were drawn to Jane, and her dormitory room soon became "an available refuge from all perplexities," according to one school friend.[12] Classmates

"BREADGIVERS"

In "Breadgivers," her class oration at the Rockford junior exhibition on April 20, 1880, Jane Addams addressed the issues of higher education for women and women's roles in modern society. Over the last half century, she told her audience, the chief focus of women's education had begun to change "from accomplishments in the arts of pleasing, to the development of . . . intellectual force and her capabilities for direct labor."

The educated young woman today, Addams asserted, "wishes not to be a man, nor like man, but she claims the same right to independent thought and action." Nonetheless, she reassured her listeners, "We still retain the old ideal of womanhood—the Saxon lady whose mission it was to give bread unto her household. So we have planned to be breadgivers throughout our lives, believing that in labor alone is happiness, and that the only true and honorable life is one filled with good works and honest toil. We will strive to idealize our labor and thus happily fulfill women's highest mission."* (Saxons were members of an ancient Germanic tribe that invaded England about 600 A.D.)

fondly recalled gathering in Jane's cramped room during their free time for debates about everything from Charles Dickens's novels to Charles Darwin's theory of evolution to women's rights. In 1909, Corinne Williams Douglas, who would go on to found a girls' school in Georgia, reminisced about Addams and their time together at Rockford:

> I see her plainly now as though it were but yesterday. The brown hair drawn back, with a decided

In his biography of Addams, Allen Davis describes Jane's junior exhibition address as "a shrewd, yet guarded declaration of independence" that "marked her first open break with the traditional role of women." Perhaps to placate the more conservative members of her audience, Addams emphasized that a woman could be a highly effective "breadgiver" in the traditional sense "as a wife, mother and homemaker," Davis writes. But, in keeping with her own plan to become a physician and work with the poor, she also implied that women could fulfill their mission as breadgivers by performing "good works and honest toil" in the public as well as the private, domestic realm, he observes.**

---

* Quoted in Gioia Diliberto, *A Useful Woman: The Early Life of Jane Addams*. New York: Scribner, 1999, pp. 73–74.
** Allen F. Davis, *American Heroine: The Life and Legend of Jane Addams*. Chicago: Ivan R. Dee, 1973, p. 20.

inclination, never encouraged, to fall apart on the side, the chin raised, the head slightly bent to one side, the face turned at an angle to me as she gave her attention to the speaker. . . . School girls are not psychologists and we never speculated as to why we liked to go to her room so that it was always crowded when the sacred "Engaged" sign was not hung out. We just knew there was always something "doing" where she was, and that however mopey it might be elsewhere there was intellectual ozone in her vicinity. But now looking back over the last thirty years, one sees that then in her little world, as now in the great world, she had the same intellectual vitality, the same cosmopolitan sympathies, the same strong self-poised character.[13]

DEVELOPING NEW INTERESTS AND ABILITIES

Throughout her four years at the seminary, Jane maintained a nearly perfect grade-point average, even with an exceptionally demanding course schedule that included two electives per semester, instead of the customary one. "Pushing against Rockford's modest academic aspirations, she was extracting all she could from the institution," author Knight writes.[14] Despite her heavy course load, Jane still took part in a broad range of extracurricular activities, including serving as president of the Literary Society, the Castalian Society (a debating club), and Rockford's first science club. As president of the class of 1881, Jane also organized the seminary's first junior class exhibition in April 1880. In addition to inviting the study body to the exhibition, Jane invited the Rockford community and press. The junior women performed an original class song and presented formal recitations and orations. Addams, in her first-ever speech before a general audience, opened the program with the main oration of the evening, the junior class address.

Of all the extracurricular activities she participated in at Rockford, the one that claimed more of Jane's time than any other was her work with the school's monthly journal, the *Rockford Seminary Magazine*. Addams began to write articles for the campus magazine during her freshman year on such diverse topics as "The Macbeth of Shakespeare" and "The Element of Hopefulness in Human Nature." By her sophomore year, she was also serving as editor of the journal's "Home Items" section, and during her junior year she took responsibility for its "Clippings and Exchanges" section. Finally, as a senior, Addams was appointed editor-in-chief. Possibly out of concern that Sill might ban her from the publication if she pushed the conservative head-mistress too far, Jane generally steered clear of controversial subjects, including women's rights, in her feature articles and editorials. According to her biographer Victoria Bissell Brown, "apart from one pro-suffrage comment," Jane avoided feminist issues altogether during the nine months that she served as editor-in-chief.[15] Nonetheless, as her senior year drew to a close in the spring of 1881, Jane was more determined than ever to pursue a professional career, instead of following the more traditional female path of marriage and motherhood.

Searching for Useful Work

On June 22, 1881, Jane Addams graduated from Rockford Female Seminary at the top of her class. She delivered a short valedictorian speech and read from her senior essay on Cassandra, the legendary Trojan prophetess, at the commencement ceremony. According to Greek mythology, Cassandra's fellow Trojans refused to listen to her when she correctly predicted Troy's defeat by the Greeks. Jane compared modern society's tendency to undervalue female powers of "intuition" and "sympathy" with the Trojans' failure to take Cassandra's warnings seriously. Cassandra's tragedy, she said, was that of women throughout the ages, to be "in the right" and yet "to be disbelieved and rejected." Reflecting her own desire to pursue a professional career and have a positive impact on society, Addams urged her classmates to use their inborn talents and strengths to help solve "social ills and social problems," instead of limiting themselves to strictly domestic concerns. Yet, as Addams would soon discover, like most of her contemporaries, her parents did not share her belief that the place for women was in the "busy, active world" every bit as much as in their traditional sphere of home and family.[1]

THWARTED AMBITION

Addams planned to spend the summer after her graduation at home, relaxing with her family, before heading off to Smith College for one year to finish her bachelor's degree. Shortly after her graduation, Rockford's trustees finally voted to turn the seminary into a degree-granting college, with the transition occurring during the 1881–1882 academic year. Anna Sill assured Addams that she had already earned the equivalent of a B.A. (Bachelor of Arts) from Rockford, although she would have to wait until June 1882 to officially receive her diploma. But Addams, apparently figuring that a B.A. from the prestigious Massachusetts college would carry more weight than one from Rockford, was still determined to go through with her original plans regarding Smith. After completing her degree requirements at Smith, she intended to enroll in medical school, possibly in Great Britain.

Upon returning to Cedarville, however, Jane quickly discovered that John Addams was as opposed to sending her to Smith as ever. Jane had always been slightly built. Her father was convinced that overwork and anxiety regarding her grades had caused Jane to become unhealthily thin by the end of her senior year at Rockford. Jane was in no condition to return to her studies anytime soon, he insisted, especially at such an academically demanding school as Smith. He would not consider letting her go to Smith until

Jane Addams, shown here at age 21, had hoped to earn a Bachelor of Arts degree at Smith College after graduating from Rockford Female Seminary. Her father, however, continued to oppose her going to Smith. Jane was torn between her duty to her family and her desire to fulfill her goals.

she had had at least one year off from studying to rest and regain her strength, he said.

Ever the dutiful daughter, Jane Addams quietly acquiesced to her father's wishes but only at a high cost to her physical and emotional health. Although she had spent most of her time at Rockford in robust good health, Jane was plagued by nearly constant exhaustion and debilitating back pain within weeks of returning home. Her father had always stressed to her that "achievement and integrity were important, that one should work hard, and do every task as well as possible," Allen Davis writes. "This sense of destiny and commitment was part of the Christian tradition, part of the Protestant ethic which was deeply rooted in American life," he notes. Yet, while John and Anna encouraged George to apply to graduate school and pursue a career in science or medicine after earning his degree from Beloit College, Jane was made to feel that her ambitious educational and career goals were ill-judged and unbecoming. "The contradiction and the conflict between the sense of destiny and belief that she could do something important, on the one hand, and the traditional role of submissive, domestic woman on the other, troubled and confounded her for years," Davis observes.[2]

A DEVASTATING LOSS

In early August 1881, Jane accompanied her parents and George on a family trip to northwestern Michigan, where John Addams wanted to explore potential investment opportunities. A few days after arriving in Michigan, however, the Addamses had to cut short their part-business, part-pleasure trip when John developed severe abdominal pain. By the time they reached Green Bay, Wisconsin, his condition had so deteriorated that he was admitted to a local hospital. Three days later, on August 17, John Addams died at the age of 59 of a burst appendix.

Jane was devastated by the loss of her beloved parent. "The poignancy of your grief arises from many causes, principally from the fact that your heart and life were wrapped

"THE RESULT IS AN UNHAPPY WOMAN"

Jane Addams was crushed by what she saw as her father's overprotectiveness and disregard for her most cherished education and career goals. A speech she later gave regarding the frustrations many educated and ambitious young women faced in the late nineteenth century sheds light on her own situation after she left Rockford in the summer of 1881. In her speech, Addams described the plight of a "typical" female graduate who leaves college full of excitement at the beginning of her adult life of "independent action." Her tradition-minded parents, however, scorn her ambition to have a career and live independently as "a foolish enthusiasm," asserting that she is merely "restless" and too young to "know what she wants." When the daughter tries to convince them otherwise, they accuse her of "setting up her will against [theirs] for selfish ends." Always taught to believe that family obligations are "sacred," the disappointed daughter "hides her hurt" and acquiesces to her parents' wish that she remain at home, under their watchful eyes, until she marries. Yet the daughter does not forget about the "great ambition in which she was thwarted," Addams told her audience. Rather, "her zeal and emotions turn inward, and the result is an unhappy woman, whose vitality is consumed by vain regrets and desires."*

---

* Quoted in Louise W. Knight, *Citizen: Jane Addams and the Struggle for Democracy*. Chicago: University of Chicago Press, 2005, p. 110.

up in your Pa," Mary's husband, John Linn, observed in a condolence note to his young sister-in-law.[3] Two weeks after her father's death, Jane confided to friend Ellen Gates Starr that she felt utterly "purposeless and without ambition. . . . Only prepare yourself so you won't be too disappointed in me when you come [to Cedarville]. The greatest sorrow that can ever come to me has passed, and I hope it is only a question of time until I get my moral purposes straightened."[4] Ellen wrote back from Chicago at once. "You are too much like your father, I think, for your 'moral purposes' to be permanently shaken by anything, even the greatest sorrow," she reassured Jane.[5] Inspired, perhaps, by Ellen's words, within a month of receiving her letter, Jane had left Cedarville for Philadelphia to begin working toward her longtime dream of earning a medical degree. Paying for her tuition at the Women's Medical School of Philadelphia was not a problem for Jane, as she was now financially independent. Her share of John Addams's large estate gave her an income of $3,000 a year, the equivalent of more than $60,000 in today's money.

PHILADELPHIA

Jane's decision to enroll at the Women's Medical School of Philadelphia in September 1881, as opposed to Smith College, as she had originally hoped to do, or one of the half-dozen other medical schools in the country that accepted female students, was probably influenced by family considerations. Anna Addams continued to have little sympathy or understanding for Jane's unconventional career goals. Anna, however, did like the idea of moving to Philadelphia with Jane, whose youth and unmarried status meant that it would be improper for her to live on her own, according to prevailing standards of behavior for women. Philadelphia appealed to Anna because it offered the promise of a more varied and sophisticated social life than little Cedarville could provide. Adding to the city's attraction for Anna was the fact that her eldest son, Harry, accompanied by his wife, Alice Addams Haldeman, had recently moved there.

Although she had been contemplating a career in medicine since she was in high school, Jane quickly became disillusioned with medical school. In truth, her literature and writing classes at Rockford had always interested her more than her science courses. Now she was bored by her entirely science-based curriculum. Nevertheless, ever the perfectionist when it came to her academic work, Jane put in long hours studying in an effort to earn the highest marks possible in her classes. Soon, however, she found herself emotionally and physically drained "by the effort to excel at something that didn't excite her," Gioia Diliberto writes.[6] In her diary, she chided herself for her "utter failure" and her inability "to work at the best of myself. . . . I am growing more sullen . . . every day."[7] Adding to Jane's frustration were her frequent clashes with Anna, who pressured her stepdaughter to accompany her on a time-consuming round of social and cultural activities, despite Jane's demanding academic schedule.

By the late winter of 1882, Jane was severely depressed and once again suffering from debilitating back pain. Urged on by Anna, she decided to drop out of medical school in March and check into Dr. Silas Weir Mitchell's Hospital of Orthopedic and Nervous Diseases in Philadelphia. Mitchell's hospital focused on treating women with neurasthenia, a psychological disorder marked by generalized aches and pains, exhaustion, depressed mood, and anxiety. Dr. Mitchell was one of the first American physicians to suggest a link between emotional stress and certain physical ailments, particularly chronic back pain. At his Philadelphia sanitarium, he emphasized complete bed rest and seclusion for his patients, with no visitors and no reading material of any sort.

Jane never commented directly on her experiences at Mitchell's Philadelphia hospital in her private or published writings. But when she returned home to Cedarville with Anna following a six-week stay there, neither her spirits nor her back pain had noticeably improved. Many years later, Jane would write movingly about the plight of a typical female college graduate torn between family demands and her drive to do something of consequence in the world. "When her health gives way under the strain, as it often does, her physician invariably advises a rest," Jane wrote. "But to be put to bed . . . is not what she requires. What she needs is simple, health-giving activity, which involves the use of all faculties." Without this type of activity, she "is restricted and unhappy; her elders, meanwhile, are unconscious of the situation, and we have all the elements of a tragedy."[8]

BACK SURGERY AND A EUROPEAN TOUR

For the next seven years after leaving Philadelphia, Jane Addams would be plagued by periods of severe depression and exhaustion as she attempted to balance her sense of obligation to her demanding stepmother and her own desire to pursue a career and have a meaningful impact on society. Soon after she and Anna returned to Cedarville in the late spring of 1882, Anna started to pressure Jane to give up her dream of having a professional career, once and for all, and get married. More specifically, she wanted Jane to marry her youngest son, George, who had developed romantic feelings for his stepsister. Twenty-one-year-old Jane, however, had not the slightest romantic interest in George, or, it would seem, in any other young man. Allen Davis thinks that, once Jane decided that she wanted a career, she ruled out marriage and motherhood for herself. In the 1880s, Davis observes, most college-educated women "believed that they could not combine marriage and a career, and in fact almost one half of the first generation of women college graduates never married."[9]

Although Jane was resolved to follow her own course when it came to marrying George, "her refusal to do her stepmother's bidding brought on waves of guilt," author Diliberto contends.[10] After a brief trip to Rockford to collect her promised Bachelor of Arts diploma from Miss Sill, Jane's emotional and physical health took a turn for the worse, and she became a virtual invalid. Deeply concerned about her younger sister, Alice persuaded Jane in late 1882 to pay a long visit to her and Harry in their new home in Mitchellville, Iowa, where Harry had begun a medical practice. Once in Mitchellville, Jane agreed to let Harry try a new German medical technique on her designed to correct curvature of the spine. The technique involved injecting an irritating solution into the tissue surrounding the spine, which would supposedly be pulled straight as the damaged tissue contracted. After several months of bed rest at Alice and Harry's house, Jane returned to Cedarville in early 1883 convinced that her back pain had been permanently reduced by the procedure.

During the spring of 1883, Jane began to make plans for an extensive tour of Western Europe. During the late 1800s, it was common for well-off young American ladies to take "grand tours" of the European continent "as a finishing touch to their education," Allen Davis notes.[11] Travel abroad was also seen as an effective remedy for depression and other forms of "nervous disease" for those women fortunate enough to afford such an expensive luxury. By the summer, Jane's ambitious travel plans had fallen into place. Accompanied by a female cousin and two friends from the Rockford Female Seminary, along with two middle-aged chaperones—the friends' aunt and Anna Addams—Jane intended to visit 10 countries over a period of nearly two years.

In late August 1883, Jane and her travel party sailed from New York for Ireland, the first stop on their grand tour. For the next 22 months, Jane studied the art and architecture of the British Isles, France, Italy, Greece, Austria, Switzerland, and Holland, among other countries, taking detailed notes in her travel journals on the magnificent paintings, sculptures, cathedrals, and castles she encountered along her way. In her journals and her letters home, she also recorded her impressions of the ordinary Europeans whose lives she observed during her travels. Some of what she saw disturbed her enormously.

Jane was particularly dismayed by her glimpses of urban poverty and working-class exploitation in two of Europe's most economically advanced and prosperous countries, Great Britain and Germany. In London, she was shocked and saddened by "the hideous human need and suffering" she witnessed in the city's destitute East End, she later recalled in her autobiography.[12] On a visit to Dresden, Germany, several weeks later, Jane angrily confronted a local brewery owner regarding his callous treatment of his female workers. The workers, who earned little more than starvation wages for their hard labor, were forced to carry heavy wooden casks of scalding beer on their backs to a "remote cooling room," Jane remembered in her autobiography. The women "were bent forward, not only under the weight which they were bearing, but because the tanks were so high that it would have been impossible for them to have lifted their heads. Their faces and hands, reddened in the cold morning air, showed clearly the white scars where they had previously been scalded by the hot stuff which splashed if they stumbled ever so little on their way." Jane's attempt to shame the brewery owner into treating his workers more humanely accomplished nothing. The owner merely responded to her reproaches with "exasperating indifference," Jane complained.[13]

This 1886 drawing from the *Illustrated London News* depicts unemployed workers applying for relief in the East End of London. During a 22-month tour of Europe in the mid-1880s, Jane Addams visited several countries in Europe. She was disheartened by the human suffering she saw among the urban poor in places like the East End.

BALTIMORE

Over the next two years after she returned from Europe in June 1885, Jane Addams spent much of her time with her stepmother in Baltimore, Maryland, where George was attending John Hopkins University as a graduate student in biology. Jane was much impressed by Baltimore's rich cultural life, particularly the excellent library, art gallery, and lecture and concert series available at the Peabody Institute, just down the street from the apartment that she and Anna rented. Yet, as Jane confided to her old friend, Ellen Gates Starr, after nearly two years abroad, she felt as much "at sea" as ever "so far as any moral purpose was concerned."[14] Nearly 25 years old, she was still searching for some sort of "useful" work, other than acting as her stepmother's companion, to fill her days and give her life meaning.[15]

While she was in Baltimore, Jane discovered that charity work was the best antidote for the depression and feelings of emptiness that had troubled her since her father's death and her withdrawal from medical school. She began to volunteer her time at a home for poor, elderly black women and an orphanage for black girls. "I had such a pleasant afternoon yesterday with the old women at the Colored Shelter," she wrote to her sister Alice, "they are so responsive and confidential and begin to know me well enough now to be perfectly free." Years later, Ellen Gates Starr told a reporter that Jane had revealed to her that, while an evening out with her well-to-do "society" acquaintances left her feeling drained, she found her visits to the impoverished residents of the old folks home and orphanage invigorating. "After a lecture or a social evening she would feel quite exhausted," Starr explained, "but after a morning with the colored people . . . she was actually physically better than if she had stayed in bed."[16]

A LIFE-CHANGING TRIP

In 1887, Jane began to plan a return trip to Europe. Her chief motivation was to help the Rockford Female Seminary. Addams had recently been named a trustee of the school, after donating $1,000 (the equivalent of more than $20,000 in today's money) to expand Rockford's book collection. Now she wanted to visit the great cities of Europe to collect high-quality reproductions of major artworks to donate to her alma mater. Jane's travel companions were to be two of her closest friends from Rockford, Ellen Gates Starr and Sarah Anderson, a young teacher at the seminary. This time around, Anna Addams chose to remain at home. But Jane, ever the dutiful stepdaughter, had no cause to worry about leaving Anna for the six months that she expected to be abroad. By the time she departed the United States for Europe in December 1887, George had decided to drop out of Johns Hopkins University and move back to Cedarville to live with his mother.

After touring France, Germany, and Italy, Jane and her friends arrived in Madrid, Spain, in April 1888. One afternoon the three women decided to attend a bullfight. Two decades later, Jane recalled the bullfight in her autobiography as one of the most important episodes, not only of her second European trip, but her entire life. Appalled by the bloody spectacle in which five bulls and even more horses were ultimately killed, Sarah and Ellen left the amphitheater in disgust before the bullfight was over. But Jane, fascinated by the violent display despite herself, stayed on to the bitter end.

Later that evening, Jane mulled over in her mind how she could have been so indifferent to the cruelty and suffering she had witnessed in the amphitheater that day. The hard questions she asked herself the night of the bullfight led to a life-changing insight, Jane wrote in *Twenty Years at Hull-House*: Since leaving school, she had deluded herself into believing that she was preparing herself for achieving something of value in the future through her world travels, studies of culture, and occasional charitable efforts. She confessed:

> It was suddenly made quite clear to me that I was lulling my conscience by a dreamer's scheme. It is easy to become the dupe of a deferred purpose, of the promise the future can never keep. . . . Nothing less than the moral reaction following the experience at a bullfight had been able to reveal to me that so far from following the wake of a chariot of

This 1865 lithograph by William Henry Lake Price depicts the Plaza de Toros of Madrid, Spain. While in the Spanish capital, Jane Addams and her two traveling companions attended a bullfight. The violence horrified her friends, who left, but Addams stayed till the end. That night, reflecting on her indifference to the cruelty of the bullfight, Addams began to ask herself some difficult questions that would change the course of her life.

philanthropic fire, I had been tied to the tail of the veriest oxcart of self seeking.[17]

By the following morning, Jane had committed herself to "a very simple plan," one that had been gradually developing in her mind for some time, she wrote in her autobiography. She would move to Chicago and rent a house in one of the city's most destitute neighborhoods. Then she would invite other young, educated middle- and upper-class women like herself, "young women who had been given over too exclusively to study," to live and work side by side with her among the impoverished laborers and their families. When Jane asked her close friend, Ellen Gates Starr, if she would help her turn what Addams referred to simply as her "scheme" into reality, Ellen enthusiastically agreed, to Jane's delight. By the time the two women left Madrid for Granada, the next stop on their tour of Spain, Jane wrote in her autobiography, "The scheme had become convincing and tangible, though hazy in detail."[18]

The Founding
of Hull House

Jane Addams spent most of June 1888 in London, investigating the city's many missions and charitable organizations before returning home to Illinois to launch her own project to improve the lives of the urban poor. She was especially eager to visit Toynbee Hall in London's destitute East End. Considered the world's first "settlement house," Toynbee Hall was founded four years earlier by Samuel Barnett, a curate in the Church of England, and his wife, Henrietta Barnett, an educator and social reformer. The Barnetts were convinced that the most effective way to help the urban lower classes lift themselves out of their grinding poverty was to "settle" among them. Moreover, when well-off volunteers actually lived among the slum dwellers they sought to help, the tremendous gulf between "haves" and "have-nots" in industrialized society would start to be bridged, they believed.

At the time that Addams first visited Toynbee Hall, the facility's live-in staff consisted of 15 men, all recent graduates of England's prestigious Oxford University. Urged on by the Barnetts, Toynbee Hall's young, upper-class residents became heavily involved in neighborhood life, running evening classes for working adults and clubs and other organized activities for children, women, new immigrants, and the elderly. They also tried to persuade local officials to provide the long-neglected East End community with better schools, a public park and library, and cleaner streets.

Toynbee Hall "is a community for University men who live there, have their recreation and clubs and society all among the poor people yet in the same style they would live in their own circle," Addams wrote to her sister Alice from England in late June 1888. "It is so far from the 'professional doing good,' so unaffectedly sincere and so productive of good results in its classes and libraries that it seems perfectly ideal," she gushed.[1] Addams's positive impression of Toynbee Hall only strengthened her conviction that, in order to have a meaningful impact on the growing scourge of urban poverty, middle- and upper-class humanitarians like herself must reside and socialize as well as work with the lower classes. Instead of following the Barnetts' example and staffing her settlement house with young male university graduates, however, Addams decided to recruit female university graduates to "settle" with her and Ellen Gates Starr in the slums of Chicago. At a time when most professions and business occupations were closed to women, Addams understood only too well the enormous frustration that many young women experienced upon leaving college. Through their involvement with the settlement house, Addams hoped, underemployed college women could

In June 1888, Jane Addams visited Toynbee Hall, considered the world's first settlement house, in the East End of London. Seeing the work done at Toynbee Hall bolstered Addams's growing belief that middle- and upper-class humanitarians must live and socialize with the urban poor to have an impact on their condition.

accomplish something useful for society and find a satisfying outlet for their talents and drive.

DRUMMING UP SUPPORT

After returning home in July, Jane spent most of the next six months attending to financial matters and visiting with her stepmother and siblings. Of all of Jane's immediate family members, only Alice was even mildly supportive of her plan to live among Chicago's underprivileged masses. Anna Addams and her two sons, Harry and George, were particularly opposed to Jane's project, which they derided as impractical, unseemly, and naive. Jane refused to be swayed by her family's criticism, however. Addams's faith in the value and ultimate success of her settlement house was unwavering, and her partner in the undertaking, Ellen Gates Starr, was just as confident.

In January 1889, Addams and Starr rented rooms in a Chicago boardinghouse and set to work drumming up financial support for their proposed settlement house. The two women first focused their efforts on the city's numerous Christian missions and churches. Within a matter of weeks, Addams and Starr's plan had won the enthusiastic backing of numerous influential religious leaders. Most of them were associated with the "social gospel movement," a liberal intellectual movement within American Protestantism that developed in the late 1800s. The social gospel movement emphasized humanitarian efforts and the brotherhood of all mankind and contended "that injustice, rather than immorality, was at least partially the cause of poverty," Gioia Diliberto explains.[2]

Addams and Starr next turned their attention to Chicago's social and economic elite. Addams, who was more comfortable with public speaking than Starr, spoke at dozens of receptions sponsored by local colleges, philanthropic groups, women's clubs, and private individuals regarding their goals for Chicago's first settlement house. She promised to make the facility "easily accessible, hospitable, tolerant in spirit," and "a place where the dependence of classes on each other would be reciprocal."[3] The two women also discussed their venture with local politicians, reporters, and school officials. "All over Chicago, as they talked and outlined their scheme, the response, especially from the younger women and men, was overwhelmingly favorable," Allen Davis writes.[4]

A PLACE TO SETTLE

Whenever they could spare time from drumming up support for their plan, Addams and Starr scoured lower-class neighborhoods in Chicago for a place to settle. Starr wrote to a friend that they hoped to find a house roomy enough to accommodate "classes or lectures or whatever we may wish" for their impoverished neighbors as well as the upper- and middle-class volunteers they expected to live with them.[5] There were plenty of locations to choose from. When Chicago was incorporated as a town in 1833, it had a population of just 350. Forty years later, the population had grown tenfold. By 1889, when Addams moved there, more than half a million people called Chicago home, a majority of them recent immigrants who worked at low-paying jobs in the city's hundreds of factories and sweat-shops. (A sweatshop is a factory or shop in which workers toil for long hours under harsh and unhealthy conditions for minimal wages.)

Finally, after five months of combing through some of Chicago's most notorious slums, Addams happened upon an elegant but run-down house at 335 Halsted Street in the West End's heavily immigrant Nineteenth Ward. Wealthy real estate entrepreneur Charles J. Hull had built the spacious brick house in 1856, when the western part of Chicago was almost completely undeveloped. Over the next decade and a half, the Nineteenth Ward became more and more industrialized. "Manufacturing establishments of every size and description, with their accompanying smells, waste products, and noise" multiplied in the area, observes author Louise Knight.[6] To Hull's dismay, the value of his stately, two-story home plummeted as cheap housing for the factories' underpaid workers sprang up in the Halsted neighborhood and floods of impoverished immigrants moved in. By 1870, Hull had fled Halsted Street for a more prosperous section of Chicago and was renting out his old home. Over the years, the house went through a series of tenants, including a charitable organization. When Addams first saw the house, a desk manufacturing company was renting most of the lower floor for storage space and offices.

In her autobiography, Addams quoted at length from a speech she gave in 1890 about Halsted Street and the Nineteenth Ward, including the area's many ethnically segregated immigrant ghettos:

> Halsted Street is thirty-two miles long, and one of the great thorough-fares of Chicago; Polk Street crosses it midway between the stockyards to the south and the shipbuilding yards on the north branch of the Chicago River. For the six miles between these two industries the street is lined with shops of butchers and grocers, with dingy . . . saloons, and pretentious establishments for the sale of ready-made clothing. . . . Between Halsted Street and the river live about ten thousand Italians. . . . To the south on Twelfth Street are many Germans, and side streets are given over almost entirely to Polish and Russian Jews. Still farther south, these Jewish colonies merge into a huge Bohemian [Czech] colony. . . . To the northwest are many Canadian-French, . . . and to the north are Irish and first-generation Americans. . . .
>
> The streets are inexpressibly dirty, the number of schools inadequate, sanitary legislation unenforced, the street lighting bad, the paving miserable and altogether lacking in the alleys and smaller streets, and the stables foul beyond description. . . .
>
> The houses of the ward, for the most part wooden, were originally built for one family and are now occupied by several. . . . Many houses have no water supply save the faucet in the back yard; there are no fire escapes.[7]

Convinced that the spacious Halsted Street house and the struggling immigrant neighborhoods surrounding it were

This photograph taken by Lewis Wickes Hine shows the living quarters of a tenement family near Hull House in Chicago. About the neighborhood surrounding Hull House, Addams wrote, "The houses of the ward, for the most part wooden, were originally built for one family and are now occupied by several."

ideal for the settlement project, Addams approached the house's current owner, Helen Culver. A wealthy woman in her own right, Culver had inherited the house and other nearby property from Charles Hull, who was her cousin. Fortunately for Addams, Culver was a philanthropist with a strong interest in helping the poor. After hearing about the settlement house plan, she agreed to rent a large first-floor room and the entire second floor to Addams for a modest monthly rate. The following spring, Culver generously offered her use of the entire house free of rent for the next four years. In gratitude, Jane decided to name the settlement Hull House, after Culver's late cousin and the house's original owner.

SERVING THE COMMUNITY

During the summer of 1889, Addams spent $1,000 of her own money to have repairs done on the house's roof and floors and to replace doors and windows. Then she decorated the graceful old house with reproductions of classic European paintings, elegant mahogany and oak furniture, delicate linens and china, and other fine objects, some gifts from friends and others belonging to her. Addams was determined to make the new house "a haven of beauty and culture" in the midst of one of Chicago's ugliest industrial slums, author Barbara Garland Polikoff writes.[8]

On September 18, Addams and Starr took up residence at 335 Halsted Street with their housekeeper, Mary Keyser. Addams later said that, when she moved into Hull House, she had no clear plan of what she would do, aside from opening the settlement house to the community for receptions, club meetings, and lectures. During the first weeks, dozens of curious neighbors visited the house. "Sweatshop workers, washerwomen, maids, factory laborers, street cleaners, taxi drivers, and peddlers—some with their entire families in tow—stopped in," Diliberto writes.[9] Soon neighborhood women began to ask if they could leave their young children at the house under Addams and Starr's supervision, while they were at work. When Jenny Dow, a well-off young Chicago woman, volunteered to organize and pay all the expenses for a day nursery and kindergarten at Hull House, Addams and Starr gratefully accepted her offer. The program was enormously popular with impoverished working women, some of whom had been reduced to leaving their little ones locked in their tenement apartment all day because they could not afford to pay a babysitter. Within a few weeks, 24 children had enrolled at the day care and 70 more names had been placed on a waiting list.

Addams and Starr gradually began to organize other community activities and services. They led separate boys' and girls' clubs and, with the help of a growing legion of volunteers, began to hold classes for adults as well as older children on a wide array of subjects including drawing, music, art history, English, American government, sewing, and cooking. Addams also organized regular social and cultural events for the neighborhood's various immigrant groups. At a time when new immigrants to the United States were expected to give up their Old World customs and values and "Americanize" as quickly as possible, she was unusually sensitive to her neighbors' deep pride in their unique cultural and ethnic heritages. Often she would devote an entire evening at Hull House to the community's large Italian population, featuring traditional Italian songs and lectures about Renaissance painting or classical Roman architecture. Other evenings at Hull House were devoted to the music, art, and history of the neighborhood's other major ethnic groups, including the Germans, Irish, Russians, Greeks, and French.

MISS KIND HEART

By the time Hull House had been open for two years, 15 residents, most of them female college graduates in their twenties or thirties, shared the old mansion with Addams and Starr. By 1895, so many women had applied to live in the settlement that a third story, capable of comfortably accommodating 25 residents, was added to Hull House. The residents were expected to contribute a small monthly fee for their room and board and donate at least two hours a week to the settlement, doing anything from kitchen work to helping out in the nursery to leading classes in art or English or cooking. (Most residents paid their own fees, often from salaries they earned as nurses, charity workers, or teachers. Other residents were supported by fellowships funded by wealthy Hull House donors.) Along with a steadily expanding group of nonresident volunteers,

A group of immigrants, ranging from children to senior citizens, sing in a Hull House choir. Classes at the settlement house included drawing, art history, English, American government, and sewing. A day nursery and a kindergarten were established, and regular social events were organized for the neighborhood's diverse immigrant groups.

the residents helped supervise 50 clubs, dozens of classes, and numerous other functions and activities for the community, including Chicago's first public playground and baths, a two-story art gallery, a gymnasium, a theater, and a coffeehouse.

Just about everyone agreed that Jane Addams was the central factor behind the new facility's enormous success. In 1892, an estimated 2,000 people were crossing the house's threshold each week, and, according to her nephew James Weber Linn:

[It] is no exaggeration to say that Jane Addams talked to most of them. . . . Jane was doing whatever part of the housework Mary Keyser left over, calling on hundreds of people in the neighborhood to interest them if she could, keeping the books as she raised the money to supplement what she and the other residents paid in, studying conditions with the care of the modern sociological scholar—ten hours a day including a hundred conferences with child, woman, man, were nothing unusual to her.[10]

The "essential fact of Hull House was the presence of Miss Addams," wrote a resident staff member, Francis Hackett. "Hull House . . . was not an institution over which

DID YOU KNOW?

Although most of Hull House's residents were single, college-educated women, the settlement house also had numerous male volunteers. Most commuted to Hull House from their homes elsewhere in Chicago or its suburbs, but a handful took up residence in Hull House. By the mid-1890s, Jane Addams had opened an annex for male residents just around the corner from the mansion, which quickly became home to a half-dozen male staff members. Hull House's first male resident was Edward Burchard, who spent several months at the settlement house following his graduation from Beloit College in 1891. When Addams published her autobiography, *Twenty Years at Hull-House*, in 1910, Burchard wrote to her that, even though the time he spent under her direction at Hull House was comparatively brief, "you more than . . . anyone else opened my mind to the realities and significance and duties of human relationships."*

* Quoted in Jean Bethke Elshtain, *Jane Addams and the Dream of American Democracy.* New York: Basic Books, 2001, p. 149.

Miss Addams presided; it was Miss Addams around whom an institution insisted on clustering."[11]

Addams quickly became known around the community for the warm and unfailingly respectful way in which she treated all of her Hull House neighbors, young and old alike. One Greek immigrant later recalled that he and his pals from the neighborhood "would walk into Hull House as though we walked into our own house. . . . Miss Addams was our mother and protector, the immigrant boy's best friend and the only one who understood us."[12] Addams "respected us" and "she respected people's traditions," remembered Ruby Delicandro, an Italian immigrant who

OTHER EARLY SETTLEMENT HOUSES IN THE UNITED STATES

Hull House was not the first settlement house in the United States. That distinction goes to the Neighborhood Guild, which opened with an all-male, college-educated staff in 1886. Organized by Stanton Coit, a leader in the Society for Ethical Culture, the Neighborhood Guild was located in Manhattan's heavily immigrant and impoverished Lower East Side. The Society for Ethical Culture had been founded 10 years earlier in New York as a religious movement aimed at promoting social justice for all people.

Just one week before Hull House officially opened in 1889, another female-led settlement house opened in New York's Lower East Side. The new facility was created by a group of Smith College graduates who called themselves the College Settlement Association. Located on Rivington Street, the College Settlement's most famous volunteer was future first lady Eleanor Roosevelt, who taught dance classes to immigrant children at the facility in 1903, when she was 19 years old.

also came to look on Hull House as her second home when she was a child growing up in the Nineteenth Ward.[13] Soon Addams's grateful neighbors on Halsted Street started to refer to her as Miss Kind Heart and Saint Jane.

Addams was always ready to help whenever an emergency arose in the neighborhood. One evening, a frantic girl came to the door of Hull House asking for Miss Addams, Jane recalled in her autobiography. An unmarried and very scared young woman in her tenement was having a baby all alone, the girl told Addams, because none of the "respectable" matrons in the building would "'touch the likes of her.'"[14] Addams called a doctor and rushed to the tenement

From 1891 to 1897, several dozen settlement houses opened in large cities throughout the United States, the best known of which was the Henry Street Settlement founded by Lillian Wald in 1893 on the Lower East Side. Born in 1867 into a well-off Jewish family, Wald was a restless young woman, like Addams, who longed to do something significant in the greater community. She attended nursing school and, in common with Addams, studied briefly at a women's medical college. In 1893, a volunteer stint teaching a health class to immigrant women on the Lower East Side persuaded Wald to move to the slum and open a settlement house modeled on Hull House. At first she focused solely on providing health care and instruction to her impoverished neighbors. But under the influence of her friend, Jane Addams, she soon expanded her services to include vocational training and recreational and cultural programs.

with Hull House resident Julia Lathrop. When the doctor was delayed, Lathrop and a very nervous Addams had to deliver the baby—a healthy boy—on their own. According to Linn, despite his aunt's insecurities regarding her medical abilities, Addams could never ignore a plea for help from a sick or injured neighbor. She "would go anywhere, quite alone, if she was summoned at three o'clock in the morning, just as if she were a doctor. She had all her life many doubts, but no fears."[15]

HULL HOUSE'S DEDICATED HELPERS

A central factor in Hull House's remarkable success was Addams's ability to attract remarkably dedicated, skilled, and well-educated volunteers. Some of the Hull House workers became Addams's lifelong friends, particularly Mary Rozet Smith, a young Chicago society woman, who contributed thousands of dollars of her own money to the facility over the years, led many children's clubs, and served as Addams's unofficial secretary. Perhaps the most influential of Hull House's talented volunteer staff, however, were two of the earliest residents, the humanitarian reformers and social activists Julia Lathrop and Florence Kelley.

Lathrop first met Addams and Ellen Gates Starr at Rockford Female Seminary, which she attended briefly before transferring to Vassar College. After college, she worked in her father's law firm as a secretary. In 1890, eager to do something more with her life, she moved to Chicago and became one of Hull House's first residents. She led several popular clubs and taught classes and, in 1893, became the first Hull House resident to be granted a state position when the governor appointed her to the Illinois State Board of Charities. She was a passionate advocate for the mentally ill, women's rights, immigrants, and child welfare, and helped create the nation's first juvenile court in Chicago in 1899. In 1912, after living at Hull House for 22 years, she left Illinois for Washington, D.C., to head the Federal

Julia Lathrop, who attended Rockford Female Seminary with Jane Addams and Ellen Gates Starr, was one of Hull House's first residents. Lathrop was a devoted advocate for women's rights, immigrants, and child welfare. She, along with Florence Kelley, helped to push Addams to take on social and economic injustice.

Children's Bureau. Lathrop retired to her hometown of Rockford, Illinois, during the early 1920s but remained involved with Hull House until her death in 1932.

Florence Kelley moved into Hull House in the winter of 1891, within months of Lathrop's arrival at the settlement house. Kelley had graduated from Cornell in Ithaca, New York, in 1876, as part of the first class at the university to include women. After leaving Cornell, she studied economics at the University of Zurich in Switzerland, became a socialist, and entered into a disastrous marriage with an abusive Russian doctor. When Kelley arrived at Hull House, she was newly single and had three young children to support.

Impressed by her passionate commitment to social justice, Addams created a job for Kelley as director of a new Hull House committee that helped young immigrant women find employment. She also arranged for Kelley's three children to live with a friend in a Chicago suburb.

Kelley had a long-standing interest in labor reform, and in 1892 she was asked by the State Bureau of Labor Statistics to study sweatshops. Her shocking exposé of the exploitative and unhealthy conditions in Chicago's sweatshops led directly to the passage of the Illinois Factory Act. At a time when many workers were compelled to toil 10 to 14 hours a day, every day of the week except Sunday, the act mandated eight-hour working days for children and women and safety rules for children working in certain industries. Soon afterward, the governor appointed Kelley as chief factory inspector for the state of Illinois. In 1899, Kelley left Hull House when she was appointed secretary of the newly formed National Consumers' League in New York City, but she retained close ties to the facility and her friend and mentor, Jane Addams.

By the time Kelley departed Hull House for New York in 1899, she, along with Lathrop, had brought about a significant change in Addams's thinking about her responsibilities toward the community. Through their own deep commitment to social investigation and activism, the two famous Hull House residents helped turn "Jane Addams from philanthropist into reformer," Allen Davis writes.[16] When Hull House first opened its door, Addams saw her role as providing cultural uplift and comfort to her destitute immigrant neighbors. As the 1890s unfolded, however, she increasingly came to view her chief task as something much bigger: helping to eliminate the poverty and inhumane working conditions that had gone hand in hand with America's rapid industrialization and urbanization over the past several decades.

America's Foremost Woman

Inspired by progressive Hull House staff members such as Florence Kelley and Julia Lathrop, Jane Addams became involved in a variety of neighborhood, citywide, and state-wide social- and political-reform causes during the decade after the settlement house's opening in 1889. Spurred on by Kelley, she campaigned for passage of the Illinois Factory Act of 1893, which mandated more humane working conditions for the state's exploited factory operatives, a ban on hiring workers under the age of 15, and an eight-hour day for women and younger teens. During the height of the crusade to get the act passed, Addams somehow found time in her hectic schedule as chief administrator of Hull House to lobby state legislators in Springfield and speak before dozens of church, social, charity, and trade union groups in support of the law. When the Illinois Supreme Court declared the Factory Act's eight-hour workday provision unconstitutional in 1895, Addams joined Kelley in fighting to have it restored. During the same period, she also devoted countless hours to helping Lathrop secure the first juvenile court system in Chicago (and the country).

DEFENDER OF ORGANIZED LABOR

During the early 1890s, Addams became increasingly focused on the issue of labor reform. She had enormous sympathy for Chicago's overworked and underpaid laborers, particularly the impoverished immigrant women and children who toiled in the Nineteenth Ward's numerous factories and sweatshops. From the start, Addams's Hull House neighbors came to her for help in handling labor disputes with exploitative employers. At first, she tried reasoning with the employers. After three neighborhood boys and Hull House club members employed by a nearby factory were injured, one of them fatally, at the same machine, Addams visited the plant owners. She felt confident that she could persuade them to take whatever steps were necessary "to prevent the recurrence of such a tragedy," Addams recalled in *Twenty Years at Hull-House*. To her dismay, however, the owners refused to spend even the relatively small sum it would have cost to add a safety guard to the dangerous machine. They insisted that the young workers' "carelessness," not their own negligence, was to blame for the horrific accidents, Addams noted in disgust.[1]

In the face of the shocking callousness and greed of some local business owners, Addams began to share the growing belief of many late-nineteenth-century American laborers that only through unionizing could they hope to secure safer working conditions and a living wage. To learn more about Chicago's budding union movement, Addams invited Mary Kenney, a local bookbindery worker and union organizer, to meet with her at Hull House. In her memoirs, Kenney confessed to being wary of Addams at first, suspecting her of being just another wealthy do-gooder with no real understanding or empathy for the worker's plight. Addams, however, quickly won over the fiery labor leader by offering to let Kenney use Hull House as a base for her all-female bookbinders union as well as for organizing other women's trade unions. Years later, Kenney fondly recalled Addams's tireless efforts on behalf of union organizing in the Nineteenth Ward. Addams not only used her own money to have union flyers printed, but she also personally distributed them around the Hull House neighborhood, Kenney wrote in her memoirs: "She climbed stairs, high and narrow. Many of the entrances were in back alleys. There were signs to 'Keep Out.' She managed to see the workers at their noon hour, and invited them to classes and meetings at Hull-House."[2]

Although Addams's support for the labor union movement met with wide approval among her working-class neighbors in the Nineteenth Ward, it shocked and angered some of Hull House's upper-class donors. Addams's outspoken support for a worker's right to organize was "unorthodox," Louise Knight notes: "Proper society thought unions to be troublemaking organizations controlled by anarchists and prone to violence."[3] A number of conservative Chicago donors stopped making contributions to the settlement house. Among them was a club of wealthy society women called the Members of the Fortnightly. By the mid-1890s, they had become convinced that Addams and her pro-labor colleagues at Hull House were "radicals," and therefore undeserving of the club's continued financial support, according to the organization's historian.[4]

ADDAMS AND THE PULLMAN STRIKE

In truth, argues historian Allen Davis, Addams was far from radical when it came to labor issues. While she strongly defended the right of unions to organize and bargain with employers, throughout her life Addams "deplored strikes and violence," he contends. Instead, Davis asserts, "she stood for arbitration, for compromise."[5] This attitude was evident in Addams's first experience with a major labor strike, the notorious Pullman strike of 1894.

Founded by George Pullman in 1867, the Pullman Palace Car Company manufactured luxury and sleeper railway cars. In 1880, Pullman opened a giant railroad factory on the southern outskirts of Chicago. He also built an adjoining company town named for himself and insisted that his workers live there. The Pullman strike began in May 1894 following a series of wage cuts and the firing of representatives from the workers' union, the American Railway Union (ARU), led by Eugene V. Debs. Pullman workers were further incensed by their boss's unwillingness, despite wage decreases averaging 25 percent, to reduce rents in his company town. In June, with the Pullman management still refusing to negotiate with the striking workers, Debs called on all ARU members to support the strikers by boycotting Pullman railway cars. Thousands of trainmen complied, bringing railway traffic out of Chicago to a virtual standstill. Because U.S. mail trains were affected by the strike, President Grover Cleveland decided to intervene. When the president sent federal troops to Chicago to suppress the strike, some strikers and their supporters were outraged. Riots, which would eventually claim at least six lives and cause hundreds of thousands of dollars in property damage, erupted. By the end of the month, the arrest of Debs and other union leaders and the disbanding of the American Railway Union had brought the bloody—and ultimately futile—strike to an end.

Riots during the Pullman strike of 1894 left six dead in Chicago and caused hundreds of thousands of dollars in property damage, such as these burned railroad cars. During the strike, Jane Addams worked to resolve the standoff. She believed that the striking workers had legitimate grievances, yet she deplored the violence that many undertook.

During the spring and early summer of 1894, several groups in Chicago had tried to mediate between Pullman officials and the strikers, including the Civic Federation of Chicago, of which Addams was a member. Addams threw herself wholeheartedly into trying to resolve the strike, even traveling alone to Pullman to investigate conditions in the company town, particularly workers' complaints regarding high rents. She and her fellow commission members strongly urged company officials to approve the creation of an impartial arbitration board to study the workers' grievances, but their pleas fell on deaf ears.

At the height of the strike-related violence in Chicago in early July 1894, Addams's beloved older sister, Mary Addams Linn, died of cancer. Jane left Hull House for Wisconsin to be with her sister's grieving family. By the time she returned in mid-July, federal troops had squelched the rioting and the strike was effectively over. Over the next few weeks, Addams gave several speeches in Chicago on the failed Pullman strike, which she eventually reworked into an article for *Survey*, a magazine for social workers. In the speeches and article, Addams went out of her way to seek the middle ground, historian Davis observes. While she staunchly supported the workers' right to organize and stressed that they had legitimate grievances against their employer, she also accused the Pullman labor movement of being "ill-directed" because it had "stirred up . . . the elements of riot and bloodshed" among the public.[6] She hoped that in the future workers and management could avoid the violence and major economic disruptions that marked the Pullman strike by committing themselves to compromise and conciliation.

GARBAGE INSPECTOR

After Mary Addams Linn's death, Jane Addams took charge of her sisters' three youngest children at the request of their overwhelmed father, John Linn. She sent the two older ones, Esther and James, off to boarding school and college, respectively, and settled the youngest, 11-year-old Stanley, with her at Hull House. Soon after Stanley moved in, however, a typhoid fever epidemic struck the Nineteenth Ward. Since Stanley's health had always been frail, Addams worried that he would be particularly susceptible to the deadly disease. Stanley's doctor agreed and urged Addams to pack

HULL HOUSE RESIDENT ALICE HAMILTON

Along with Florence Kelley and Julia Lathrop, one of the most famous and influential women ever to live in Hull House was Alice Hamilton. A graduate of the University of Michigan Medical School, Hamilton moved into the settlement house in 1898, after accepting a professorship at the Women's Medical School of Northwestern University.

When she was not working at her day job, Hamilton ran a well baby clinic at Hull House to provide routine medical care to neighborhood children. During a typhoid fever epidemic that swept the neighborhood in 1902, Hamilton was able to show a direct link between inadequate sewage disposal and the spread of the disease, prompting a major reorganization of the Chicago Health Department. As she got to know the families in the Halsted neighborhood, Hamilton came to realize that many of their health problems were linked to

One of the most influential women to have been a Hull House volunteer was Alice Hamilton, who moved into the settlement house in 1898. Hamilton did extensive work in linking the health problems of the urban poor to unhealthy working conditions. In 1919, she became a professor of industrial medicine at Harvard University, the school's first female faculty member.

(continues)

(continued)

unhealthy working conditions, including exposure to noxious chemicals. This inspired her to participate in the Occupational Diseases Commission, a special committee appointed by the governor of Illinois in 1910 to study unhealthy work practices in the state. As a consequence of the commission's findings, the state legislature passed several groundbreaking workers' compensation laws for industrial employees who suffered job-related health impairment or injuries.

From 1911 to 1920, using Hull House as her home base, Hamilton investigated industrial health hazards at the national level for the U.S. Bureau of Labor. In 1919, she finally moved out of Hull House to become Harvard University's first female faculty member. But her appointment as professor of industrial medicine at Harvard Medical School did not end her long relationship with Jane Addams and her settlement house. Every spring until Addams's death in 1935, Hamilton traveled back to Chicago from Cambridge, Massachusetts, to live and work at Hull House for three months.

the boy off to boarding school in the suburbs, where the air and drinking water were much cleaner and healthier than in the garbage-strewn and rat-infested Nineteenth Ward.

Addams hated to send away Stanley, who had been hit hard by the loss of his mother, but she believed she had no choice given the putrid, disease-breeding conditions in the Hull House neighborhood. Her own despair regarding her young nephew in the summer of 1894 helped her to truly understand for the first time what neighborhood parents who lacked the financial means to send their ailing children off to healthier environments must be suffering. Racked by guilt, she resolved to wage war on the Nineteenth Ward's squalor. In *Twenty Years at Hull-House*, she recalled feeling "ashamed that other delicate children who were torn from their families, not into boarding school but into eternity, had not long before driven me to effective action."[7]

Since Hull House opened in 1889, Addams and her colleagues at the settlement house had been protesting to city officials regarding the haphazard garbage pickup in the neighborhood. City Hall, however, had consistently turned a deaf ear to their complaints. In the summer of 1894, Addams decided that the most effective way to get City Hall's attention would be to have a volunteer investigative team scour the alleys and streets of the Halsted neighborhood, recording every health violation it encountered. In just two months, team members compiled a list of more than 1,000 violations. These included scores of missing or perpetually overflowing outdoor garbage bins by apartment buildings and businesses, horse and other animal carcasses left to rot on the street, and sidewalks buried beneath as much as a foot-and-a-half of compacted refuse. Yet, even after Addams presented the team's shocking findings to City Hall, government officials refused to take action.

Finally, in desperation, Addams resolved to apply for a contract to collect the garbage herself for the Hull House neighborhood to ensure the job was properly done. Addams's plan to clean up Halsted Street put her in direct conflict with the ward's corrupt alderman, Johnny Powers. According to the slang of the time, Powers was a "boodler," a political "boss" who specialized in bribery, cronyism, and shady backroom deals. Powers had always arranged for garbage collection contracts in the Nineteenth Ward to go to his cronies. In return for their support at the polls—and perhaps a kickback—Powers looked the other way when his handpicked collectors failed to do their job properly. Largely owing to Powers's efforts, Addams's bid for a collection contract was turned down. To Addams's surprise, though, in the spring of 1895 Chicago's new reform-minded mayor, George Swift, named her garbage inspector for the entire Nineteenth Ward, the first time a woman had ever been appointed to such a position in the city. As garbage inspector, it was Addams's responsibility to ensure that all dwellings and businesses in the ward had a garbage bin, that collectors emptied bins regularly and completely, and that streets, sidewalks, and alleys were kept free of trash and debris.

Addams took her new job seriously. Every morning she followed the garbage wagons in her horse-drawn buggy as the collectors wended their way through the Nineteenth Ward to ensure that they completed their duties to her satisfaction. She quickly decided that the number of garbage crews assigned to the ward was inadequate and petitioned City Hall to provide additional ones. She also insisted that animal carcasses be promptly removed from streets, pushed City Hall to pave all of the ward's alleys, and took landlords to court for failing to provide enough garbage bins for their buildings. After several months on the job, Addams turned over her duties to Hull House resident Amanda Johnson, confident that her efforts had made a real difference in cleaning up the ward. Some of Addams's more traditional immigrant neighbors were dismayed by her willingness to take on what they considered a man's job. But her unconventional stint as a city garbage inspector brought her—and Hull House—more favorable publicity than they had ever received. The Chicago press "was charmed by the image of a courageous little woman battling the conniving politicians to protect the health of innocent people," Gioia Diliberto notes.[8] Gushed one admiring newspaper reporter, "Miss Addams has achieved wonders in the ward."[9]

GOING AFTER JOHNNY POWERS

Addams's success at cleaning up the Nineteenth Ward's garbage-strewn streets inspired her to try to clean up its corrupt politics as well. In 1896, she began what would turn out to be a two-year campaign to oust Alderman Johnny Powers from office. Powers's apparent indifference to the ward's unsanitary conditions—and the high disease and death rates that went along with them—dismayed Addams, as did his habit of blocking virtually every effort at reform that she and her Hull House colleagues made in the neighborhood. For example, when the Hull House staff tried to get the school board to replace a run-down, overcrowded public school attended primarily by the children of recent immigrants, Powers crushed the project because most of the students' parents could not vote. Instead, he proposed using tax money to construct a new parochial school that would serve the children of his tried-and-true supporters at the polls.

Aldermen were elected to two-year terms in Chicago, and in the spring of 1896, Powers came up for re-election. Addams, along with Florence Kelley and other Hull House reformers, persuaded William Gleeson, a member of the Hull House Men's Club and the president of the Chicago Bricklayers' Union, to run for Powers's seat. When Election Day rolled around in April, however, the flashy and smooth-talking incumbent beat Addams's reform-minded candidate by a landslide. Despite his well-founded reputation for taking bribes and kickbacks, Powers was popular in the Nineteenth Ward. In common with other inner-city political bosses of the era, Powers ingratiated himself with his impoverished, immigrant constituents by doing personal favors for them such as helping them get jobs or bailing them out of jail. He also regularly handed out modest but much appreciated gifts to Nineteenth Ward residents, ranging from free railroad passes to turkeys at Thanksgiving.

Voters were particularly impressed by Powers's generosity and sensitivity in covering the funeral expenses of his poorest constituents so that the deceased's family could avoid the disgrace of having their loved one buried by the county. Indeed, Powers attended and helped pay for his constituents' wakes and funerals so frequently that he earned the nickname "The Great Mourner."

In 1898, after Powers maneuvered to have Hull House resident Amanda Johnson removed from her position as garbage inspector and replaced by one of his cronies, Addams resolved to try again to bring down the Nineteenth Ward's "boodling" alderman. This time she and her Hull House colleagues chose longtime ward resident and Hull House volunteer Simeon Armstrong as their candidate. Throwing herself wholeheartedly into the campaign to unseat Powers, Addams put in long hours raising funds for Armstrong, distributing campaign posters and handbills, and giving interviews to Chicago newspapers about Powers's corrupt and self-serving ways. For what may have been the first time ever in his political career, Powers was running scared. He and his supporters accused Addams and her fellow female crusaders at Hull House of wanting to impose "petticoat government" on the Nineteenth Ward, and, during the final weeks of the campaign, they allegedly handed out more than $10,000 in bribes to constituents and several hundred kegs of free beer.[10] As it turned out, Powers had nothing to worry about. Just as he had in 1896, he trounced the Hull House candidate at the polls. "I may not be the sort of man the reformers like, but I am what my people like," Powers once said regarding his enduring popularity in the Nineteenth Ward.[11]

A NATIONAL REPUTATION

Although Florence Kelley urged Addams to continue the campaign to oust Powers in the 1900 election, Addams was unwilling to waste any more time or energy going after the beloved alderman. Moreover, writes Diliberto, Addams's long struggle with the boodling ward boss "had convinced her that life on Halsted Street would never improve without larger citywide and national reforms. She was developing a broad vision of the roots of poverty as sprouting from deep injustice at the core of American life."[12] By the start of the new century, Addams was increasingly using her considerable talents as a writer and a public speaker to bring her social reform views and activities into the national spotlight. In the process, she would become one of the leading figures in the Progressive movement, a loosely knit coalition of chiefly middle- and upper-class reformers dedicated to creating a more just and humane society, as well as one of the best known and admired women in all of America.

DID YOU KNOW?

In 1900, Jane Addams decided to set aside a room at Hull House as a Labor Museum, where the traditional skills of pottery, weaving, basket-making, woodworking, metalworking, and embroidery that immigrants brought over with them from their native countries or ethnic groups could be demonstrated, preserved, and celebrated. Addams realized that many of the Americanized children of immigrant parents failed to appreciate, and, in some cases, were even ashamed of, the older generation's rich cultural legacy. According to author Barbara Garland Polikoff, the Labor Museum, which quickly became one of Hull House's most popular features, was "the first such endeavor in the United States to recognize the value of the arts and crafts of immigrant artisans."*

---

* Barbara Garland Polikoff, *With One Bold Act: The Story of Jane Addams*. Chicago: Boswell, Books 1999, p. 161.

By 1910, Hull House had grown into a complex of several interconnected buildings. Dignitaries like President Theodore Roosevelt visited Hull House to meet Jane Addams, who was becoming one of the country's most famous and admired social reformers.

Between 1895, when she published her first book, *Hull-House Maps and Papers*, and her death 40 years later, Addams published 11 books and more than 500 articles for a variety of magazines, journals, and newspapers, including such prestigious publications as the *American Journal of Sociology* and the *Atlantic Monthly*. By far her most popular book was her autobiography, *Twenty Years at Hull-House*, published in 1910. During the early 1900s, Addams found herself in high demand as a speaker as well as a writer, and she criss-crossed the country giving lectures on her favorite causes, from child labor reform to unionization to childhood education. Soon, luminaries from around the nation and the world were flocking to Hull House to meet Addams, including American educational reformer and philosopher John Dewey; Prime Minister James Ramsay MacDonald of Great Britain; Prince Peter Kropotkin of Russia; Queen Marie of Romania; and U.S. President Theodore ("Teddy") Roosevelt.

In recognition of her status as one of the country's most famous and respected social reformers, Addams received many important honors during the first years of the twentieth century. These included her election as the first female president of the National Conference of Social Work in 1909 and honorary degrees from Smith College and Yale University in 1910 (the first woman in Yale's history to be so honored). In 1911, she was also appointed as the first head of the newly created National Federation of Settlement and Neighborhood Centers and the following year was named "America's Foremost Woman" by *American Magazine*. Lauded in countless periodical and newspaper articles as the closest thing the United States had to a homegrown saint, in the minds of many of her countrymen, Addams came to represent "the American virtues of 'benevolence,' 'disinterested conduct,' and 'redeeming love,'" Allen Davis writes. "She was a symbol of the best of American democracy, . . . who . . . assured everyone that despite poverty and tragedy everywhere, in the end right would prevail."[13]

Saint Jane Becomes Controversial

By the end of the first decade of the twentieth century, Hull House had grown to include more than a dozen interconnected buildings, and its director and cofounder, Jane Addams, had become one of the most respected and admired women in America. Little could anyone have imagined that within a few short years the beloved charity worker, social activist, and author would find herself the object of widespread public scorn.

THE PRESIDENTIAL CAMPAIGN OF 1912

In 1912, Addams became actively involved in partisan politics at the national level for the first time when she backed her friend and fellow reformer, Theodore Roosevelt, in his bid to regain the presidency. Roosevelt, who had served as the twenty-sixth president of the United States from 1901 to 1909, was the most celebrated and influential member of the Republican Party's progressive, or reformist, wing. At the end of his second term in office, Roosevelt decided to retire from politics and support fellow Republican William Howard Taft for the presidency. In 1912, though, disappointed by what Roosevelt viewed as Taft's lukewarm commitment to reform, Roosevelt challenged the incumbent president for their party's nomination. When the conservative-controlled Republican convention passed him over for Taft, Roosevelt broke with his longtime party to found the Progressive, or "Bull Moose," Party. Soon afterward, he asked Addams to support his presidential candidacy under the Progressive banner.

At Roosevelt's invitation, during the summer of 1912, Addams helped formulate the new Progressive Party platform, which stressed social, industrial, and political reform, including the regulation of conditions and hours for workers, particularly children and women, and woman suffrage. Like many social justice activists and social workers in 1912, Addams was thrilled by what she called the Progressives' "splendid platform." On August 7, she enthusiastically seconded Roosevelt's nomination for president at the party's convention in Chicago, where convention-goers applauded her nearly as long and as loudly as they had applauded the candidate himself. In her nominating speech, Addams expressed her deep admiration for the Progressive Party's humanitarian and broad-minded agenda:

> A great party has pledged itself to the protection of children, to the care of the aged, to the relief of overworked girls, to the safeguarding of burdened men. Committed to these human undertakings, it is inevitable that such a party should appeal to women, should seek to draw upon the great reservoir of their

In 1912, Jane Addams backed Theodore Roosevelt in his third-party bid to win back the U.S. presidency. Roosevelt, who had been president from 1901 to 1909 as a Republican, ran as the nominee of the Progressive Party. Addams was instrumental in writing the party's platform.

moral energy so long undesired and unutilized in practical politics.[1]

Addams's one major area of disagreement with Roosevelt at the 1912 convention concerned his treatment of African-American party members. A staunch supporter of racial equality, in 1909 Addams had helped found the leading black civil rights organization of the twentieth century, the National Association for the Advancement of Colored People (NAACP), and soon after was elected to its executive committee. She was dismayed when Roosevelt, fearful of losing white voters in the strongly segregationist South, refused to seat black delegates from Mississippi and Florida or support her efforts to include a platform plank guaranteeing equal rights to African Americans. Addams seriously considered breaking with Roosevelt over the race issue. In the end, though, she swallowed her misgivings and stuck by Roosevelt and the Progressive Party. "Imbedded in this new movement is a strong ethical motive," Addams explained in an editorial for the NAACP's monthly periodical, *The Crisis*. Consequently, once in power, the Progressives were "bound to lift this question of the races . . . out of the grip of the past and into a new era of solution," she optimistically declared.[2]

During the autumn of 1912, Addams campaigned tirelessly for Roosevelt all over the United States, drawing large and enthusiastic crowds wherever she spoke. "Wherever I went I heard nothing but talk of Jane Addams," women's rights activist and Roosevelt supporter Anna Howard Shaw remarked. "I suppose other political speakers had been out there, but you never would have guessed it from what people had to say."[3] Political pundits predicted that Addams's endorsement was worth at least a million votes to Roosevelt. On Election Day, however, Democrat Woodrow Wilson soundly defeated both Roosevelt and Taft. Addams refused to be discouraged by the election results. She comforted herself with the thought that the Progressive platform she had helped write had brought unprecedented public attention to such worthwhile causes as labor reform and female suffrage. Although some people criticized Addams's willingness to become involved in the cutthroat world of partisan politics as unseemly behavior for a woman, most Americans continued to hold "Saint Jane" in the highest esteem after the 1912 presidential election. "Indeed, on the

WOMEN'S VOTING RIGHTS

Although Jane Addams was a longtime supporter of women's rights, she did not join the organized suffrage movement until comparatively late, attending her first national suffrage meeting, a National American Woman Suffrage Association (NAWSA) convention, in 1906. (The organized movement to gain full voting rights for American women had begun in 1869 with the founding of NAWSA by Susan B. Anthony and Elizabeth Cady Stanton and would last until 1920, when female suffrage was finally achieved through the Nineteenth Amendment to the U.S. Constitution.) "Jane was a latecomer to organized suffrage," Gioia Diliberto explains, "because she believed other issues— child labor, unions, sanitation, and factory regulation, to name a few—were more pressing."* When the campaign for woman suffrage began to gain momentum during the early years of the twentieth century, however, Addams decided that she must take a public stand on female voting rights.

In 1911, Addams was chosen to serve as NAWSA's first vice president, a position she held for the next three years. During

eve of the outbreak of World War I [August 1914] she was at the peak of her reputation, internationally known as the best representative of American womanhood and symbol of the American spirit of equality and justice for all people," historian Davis writes.[4]

THE OUTBREAK OF WORLD WAR I

After World War I erupted in Europe in 1914, Addams became as focused on promoting the cause of world peace

those years, she crisscrossed the country giving public lectures in favor of suffrage, and in 1913 she attracted worldwide attention when she traveled to Hungary to speak at a convention of the International Woman Suffrage Alliance held in Budapest. In contrast to some American suffrage leaders, who only wanted upper- and middle-class women to receive the vote—ostensibly to counterbalance the substantial male immigrant vote—Addams supported giving the vote to women from all socio-economic classes. She was convinced that working-class and immigrant women could be relied on to cast their votes intelligently, "and, what was more important, they needed the vote to protect themselves and their families from being exploited by government and society," historian Allen Davis writes.**

---

* Gioia Diliberto, *A Useful Woman: The Early Life of Jane Addams.* New York: Scribner, 1999, p. 221.

** Allen F. Davis, *American Heroine: The Life and Legend of Jane Addams.* Chicago: Ivan R. Dee, p. 187.

as she had been on promoting industrial and social reform. Addams had a long-standing interest in pacifism, influenced in part by her admiration for the Russian writer and fervent pacifist Leo Tolstoy, whom she met on a trip to Europe in 1896. As early as seven years before the start of World War I, Addams had written a book on her pacifist beliefs entitled *Newer Ideals of Peace.* Based on a series of lectures she gave at the University of Wisconsin in 1906, *Newer Ideals of Peace* argued that ethnically diverse communities, such as the Hull House neighborhood, could help bring about world peace by encouraging international and interethnic understanding. The book also stressed that freedom from war and social justice went hand in hand—in the absence of peace, the ideals of social justice could never be fully realized, Addams maintained.

When Germany declared war on Russia on August 1, 1914, sparking an extraordinarily deadly and destructive conflict that rapidly came to involve almost every major European power, Addams turned her attention to the issue of world peace with a new sense of urgency. She lost no time in taking a public stand against the quickly widening war, joining more than 1,000 other female peace demonstrators in parading down New York City's Fifth Avenue that month to show her disapproval for the fighting. Working closely with other women in the social justice movement as well as suffragists such as Carrie Chapman Catt, Addams focused on organizing American women against what would soon come to be known as the "Great War." Women were the natural enemies of violence and war, Addams repeatedly asserted, because they were the ones who brought new life into the world and were nurturing by instinct.

By late 1914, the women's antiwar movement in the United States had grown to the point that Addams and Catt decided to call a national conference of female peace activists in Washington, D.C., for the following January.

The conference, which Addams chaired, attracted more than 3,000 women from across the country. By its end, the attendees had decided to found a new political party, the Women's Peace Party, and had elected Addams as its head. The Peace Platform adopted by the new party in January 1915 urged the neutral nations, and particularly the most powerful one of all, the United States, to offer "continuous mediation" to the warring nations until the conflict was peacefully resolved. (By continuous mediation, Addams and her fellow Peace Party members meant that the warring nations would continuously bring their differences and demands to a panel of mediators from the neutral nations until a peace settlement could be hammered out.) The preamble, or introduction, to the Peace Platform declared:

> We, women of the United States, assembled in behalf of World Peace, grateful for the security of our own country, but sorrowing for the misery of all involved in the present struggle among warring nations, do hereby band ourselves together to demand that war be abolished. . . . We demand that women be given a share in deciding between war and peace in all the courts of high debate—within the home, the school, the church, the industrial order and the state.[5]

INTERNATIONAL PEACE ACTIVIST

Soon after the conference in Washington, D.C., Dutch physician, suffragist, and peace activist Aletta Jacobs contacted Addams. Jacobs was organizing an International Peace Congress of Women to be held at The Hague in the Netherlands at the end of April, and she wanted Addams and other delegates from the Women's Peace Party to attend.

Because of Addams's status as the largest neutral nation's most famous female pacifist, Jacobs also invited Addams to chair the congress. Although still grieving the recent

Jane Addams *(second from left)* was among the U.S. contingent of peace activists traveling in April 1915 to participate in the International Peace Congress of Women at The Hague in the Netherlands. After the United States entered World War I, Addams's peace activism earned her widespread public scorn.

death of her last surviving sister, Alice, Addams dutifully set sail for the Netherlands on April 16, accompanied by her close friend and fellow Hull House resident Alice Hamilton. More than 1,300 women from a dozen countries, including all the warring nations and many of the neutral ones in Europe, flocked to The Hague to protest the Great War. The congress's diverse delegates founded the International Women's Committee (later renamed the Women's International League for Peace and Freedom) and promptly elected Addams as the new organization's first president.

As president of the International Women's Committee, Addams played a pivotal role in formulating the set of 20 proposals issued by the group in early May 1915. Some of the proposals were intended to end the current fighting, while others were aimed at preventing future wars. A key demand of the committee was that the neutral nations pressure Germany, Austria-Hungary, Turkey, Great Britain, France, and the other belligerents to declare a cease-fire and begin continuous mediation under their direction at once. The women also called for the creation of a permanent international court to mediate developing international disputes before they escalated into armed conflicts; worldwide disarmament; self-rule for all national groups; complete freedom of the seas and of trade; and universal female suffrage. The committee voted to send representatives immediately to government leaders in the warring and neutral European nations and to President Woodrow Wilson to discuss their proposals with them. It was decided that Addams and Jacobs, with Alice Hamilton as an unofficial delegate, would visit the warring countries, while another small international delegation would carry the congress's message of continual mediation to the leading neutral countries of Europe.

In May and June 1915, Addams and Jacobs visited the capitals of Great Britain, Austria, Hungary, Germany, France, and Italy, which had joined the war in late April on the Allied side. (In World War I, the Allies—chiefly Great Britain, France, Russia, Italy, and, from April 1917 on, the United States—were pitted against the Central Powers—primarily Germany, Austria-Hungary, and Turkey.) The two women were received respectfully by government officials from the warring nations, but Addams was disappointed by the leaders' unwillingness to engage in peace negotiations, despite the tens of thousands of lives already lost in the conflict. In July, Addams sailed home to the United States, resolved to speak personally with Woodrow Wilson about initiating a mediation conference with the belligerents. Although she had campaigned for Roosevelt in the 1912 presidential campaign, over the past three years, she had come to respect Wilson, who had embraced many of the same social reforms that she had helped to write into the Progressive Party's platform.

FALL FROM GRACE

On July 9, 1915, a few days after arriving in New York from Great Britain, Addams spoke before a large group of pacifists at Carnegie Hall in Manhattan regarding her experiences overseas. Toward the end of her speech, she unintentionally dropped a bombshell when she said that many of the young European soldiers she met near the front lines were so disturbed by the brutality of bayonet fighting that they had to numb themselves with rum or absinthe before going into battle. To her chagrin, reporters covering the speech sensationalized her claims that some soldiers turned to alcohol to blunt the horror of bayonet charges, while all but ignoring the rest of her comments, including her observations regarding the tremendous toll the war was taking on the people of Europe. "TROOPS DRINK-CRAZED, SAYS MISS ADDAMS," a typical headline blared the morning after her speech at Carnegie Hall.[6] Over the next days and weeks, newspaper editorials across the nation blasted the woman once revered as America's only homegrown saint as ignorant and insensitive; ordinary citizens sent Addams irate letters; and even Teddy Roosevelt, a fervent supporter of the Allied cause, turned on his longtime friend, publicly ridiculing her as "poor bleeding Jane" and "one of the shrieking sisterhood."[7] Addams's remarks "had struck at a sacred myth, the myth that the soldier fought and died because of his sense of duty and his love of country," explains Allen Davis, and "the myth of the brave and gallant soldier was close to the heart of many Americans."[8]

The scathing editorials and letters that followed in the wake of Addams's Carnegie Hall remarks in 1915 paled next to the widespread public hostility she encountered after the United States finally entered World War I on the Allied side in early April 1917. Over the previous two years, Addams had devoted herself to the cause of world peace, participating in rallies, giving lectures, and writing many articles on the subject. She also met twice with Woodrow Wilson in 1915 and early 1916 to urge him to take the lead in organizing an international peace conference of the neutral nations. Although Wilson rejected her request to arrange a meeting of the neutral countries, Addams was encouraged by his ongoing commitment to keeping the United States out of the war. Then, in February 1917, Germany resumed unrestricted submarine warfare on neutral merchant and passenger vessels in the Atlantic Ocean, a highly controversial policy it had abandoned a year earlier under strong pressure from the American government. During the late winter of 1917, dozens of American lives were lost as a result of unprovoked German U-boat attacks on neutral vessels in the Atlantic, inflaming public opinion against Berlin. Americans were further enraged when reports surfaced in March that Berlin had secretly approached Mexican officials about declaring war against the United States should Washington decide to enter World War I on the Allied side. By April 2, when Wilson formally asked Congress to declare war on Germany, he—along with a majority of the American public—had concluded that neutrality was no longer an option for the United States. Four days later, on April 6, 1917, Congress voted overwhelmingly in favor of Wilson's request for a declaration of war.

"The entry of the U.S. into the war presented the greatest challenge to Jane Addams's pacifist ideals that she had yet encountered," author Barbara Garland Polikoff observes.[9] Addams found herself harshly criticized not only by the press but also by many of her colleagues in the social justice movement, even those who had joined her in publicly opposing the war before April 1917. Denounced

IN HER OWN WORDS

In her book, *Peace and Bread in Time of War*, published in 1922, four years after the end of World War I, Jane Addams recalled the enormous emotional toll that public disapproval of her anti-war stance took on her:

> I experienced a bald sense of social opprobrium and wide-spread misunderstanding which brought me very near to self-pity, perhaps the lowest pit into which human nature can sink. Indeed the pacifist in war time, with his precious cause in the keeping of those who control the sources of publicity and consider it a patriotic duty to make all types of peace propaganda obnoxious, constantly faces two dangers. Strangely enough he finds it possible to travel from the mire of self-pity straight to the barren hills of self-righteousness and to hate himself equally in both places.
>
> From the very beginning of the great war, as the members of our group gradually became defined from the rest of the community, each one felt increasingly the sense of isolation, which rapidly developed after the United States entered the war into that destroying effect of "aloneness." . . . We never ceased to miss the unquestioning comradeship experienced by our fellow citizens during the war. . . . Solitude has always had its demons, harder to withstand than the snares of the world.*

---

* Quoted in Barbara Garland Polikoff, *With One Bold Act: The Story of Jane Addams*. Chicago: Boswell Books, 1999, pp. 182–83.

on all sides, Addams was expelled from the Daughters of the American Revolution (an organization for the female descendants of individuals who helped win American independence) and barred from speaking before many colleges, charitable organizations, and women's clubs across the nation. Yet, although Addams's speaking fees had been her chief source of income for decades, she held fast to her convictions.

On November 11, 1918, Germany finally signed an armistice with the Allied powers, bringing the war to an end. An estimated 10 million soldiers had died and twice that many were wounded over the course of four agonizing years of fighting. Among the dead was Addams's nephew John Linn, the son of her beloved older sister, Mary. A U.S. Army chaplain, John Linn fell at the Battle of the Argonne in France in October 1918, barely one month before the cease-fire. Her nephew's death devastated Addams. But it also made her more committed than ever to her international crusade for a permanent peace, a crusade that would remain a focal point of her life right up until her last days.

Final Years
And Legacy

During the spring of 1919, while negotiators for the victorious Allies were hammering out peace terms with Germany and the other Central Powers in Paris, the newly created Women's International League for Peace and Freedom or WILPF (formerly the International Women's Committee) was meeting in Zurich, Switzerland. In recognition of her unwavering commitment to pacifism, Jane Addams was unanimously elected as WILPF's first president. In June 1919, shortly before the signing of the Treaty of Versailles between the Allies and Germany, the leading Central Power, WILPF passed a resolution condemning the settlement as one-sided and unnecessarily harsh, and warning that the punitive treaty would sow the seeds for another world war. Soon after, Addams traveled to Paris to present the league's resolution on the Treaty of Versailles to Woodrow Wilson, one of the agreement's chief authors. To Addams's disappointment, the president declined to meet with her in person, instead shunting her off to one of his aides.

POSTWAR ATTACKS ON JANE ADDAMS

During the spring of 1919, Addams and Alice Hamilton had volunteered to help an American mission funded by the pacifistic Society of Friends (otherwise known as the Quakers) deliver $30,000 worth of food to war-ravaged Germany. At the insistence of the U.S. government, the humanitarian mission was barred from entering Germany until its leaders ratified the Treaty of Versailles, however. In early July 1919, shortly after the formal signing of the treaty at the Palace of Versailles near Paris, Addams and Hamilton traveled to Germany on the first civilian passports granted to Americans following World War I. The two women were appalled by the widespread hunger they observed in Germany, particularly among the nation's youngest—and most vulnerable—citizens. At Leipzig, Frankfurt, Berlin, and dozens of smaller cities and villages, Addams encountered emaciated children forced to survive on little more than "war-soup" made from "wheat or rye flour, and sawdust, stirred into a pint of hot water," she reported to her nephew, James Weber Linn.[1]

Addams was determined that Americans should know about postwar Germany's humanitarian crisis. On returning home to the United States in August, she lectured extensively on the malnourished boys and girls she had observed almost everywhere she went in Germany and pled for donations to feed these innocent victims of war. To Addams's surprise and dismay, many Americans reacted negatively to her humanitarian campaign on behalf of Germany's starving children. They viewed her preoccupation with the suffering of Germans as inappropriate in light of the fact that Central Power forces had killed or wounded some 325,000 U.S. soldiers during the Great War. They accused her of caring more about America's former enemies than she did about

ELLEN GATES STARR

Hull House's cofounder, Ellen Gates Starr, lived there until 1920, although she was a frequent visitor to the settlement house for most of the 1920s. In 1929, after she was left paralyzed below the waist following surgery on her spine, she took up residence in a Catholic convent in Suffern, New York, where she died in 1940 at age 80. During her four decades at Hull House, Starr organized clubs, taught classes, and ran a bookbindery. She also spent much of her time crusading for better working conditions for women and children. She was involved in many labor protests in

During her three decades at Hull House, cofounder Ellen Gates Starr advocated for better working conditions for women and children, participating in numerous labor protests.

Chicago over the years and was charged with disorderly conduct for picketing Henrici's, a local restaurant, with a group

her own countrymen. British suffragist and lecturer Maude Royden reported that, when she toured the United States in the early 1920s, she was stunned by how "swiftly and completely" Addams's "popularity had vanished" since her last visit to America shortly before World War I erupted. On

of striking waitresses in 1914. In 1916, she joined the Socialist Labor Party and, although American women would not be granted the right to vote for several more years, Starr ran for alderman in the Nineteenth Ward that year. She was defeated.

Although Starr always insisted that she did not feel that she had been pushed into the background by Addams at the institution she cofounded, some of her letters indicate that she was jealous of Addams. For example, Starr took a leading role in helping to publicize and raise money for the garment strike of 1910 in Chicago. After the strike was over, the victorious garment workers paraded up Halsted Street, passing right in front of Hull House. "I was leaning out of my window all the time, recognizing my friends, waving to them, throwing kisses to the girls I know," Starr wrote to her father. "The men took off their hats to me & waved them, & cheered. It was great. I never had such an experience. They cheered the house three or four times, & Jane once, rather feebly. She said to me afterward, 'I am glad they cheered the house.' And I didn't say, 'I suppose you know why.'"*

---

* Quoted in Gioia Diliberto, *A Useful Woman: The Early Life of Jane Addams*. New York: Scribner, 1999, p. 246.

her first visit to the United States, the mention of Addams's name inevitably brought "a storm of applause" from her audiences, Royden wrote.[2] On her postwar American speaking tour, however, most audiences greeted the name of Addams with a stony silence, she recalled.

Addams's humanitarian crusade to win public sympathy and financial assistance for German war victims was not the only cause of her continuing unpopularity at home after World War I. Addams also found herself a target of the anti-Red (anticommunist) hysteria that gripped the United States from the war's end through the early 1920s. The so-called Red Scare grew from widespread fears that leftist subversives inspired by the Communist Bolshevik Revolution of 1917 in Russia were plotting to overthrow the U.S. government. Americans with known or suspected left-wing sympathies were accused of being Communist agents, and many innocent people were arrested, detained, or deported. Addams's ties to left-leaning labor unions and her willingness to allow people of all political views, including socialists, Communists, and anarchists, to hold meetings and speak at Hull House made her vulnerable to accusations that she was a secret radical. *Scabbard and Blade*, the publication of the Honorary Society of the ROTC (Reserve Officers' Training Corps), even went so far as to denounce Addams as "the most dangerous woman in America."[3] Throughout the early 1920s, Addams's name also appeared prominently on "spider-web charts" created by the War Department and various conservative groups such as the Daughters of the American Revolution. These diagrams attempted to show a tangled, Bolshevik-inspired conspiracy of feminist, pacifist, socialist, and pro-labor individuals and organizations aiming to take control of the country. Addams "was a convenient symbol to attack," Allen Davis observes, "because she was the most famous woman in America, formerly admired and now fallen from grace."[4] She also supported, and in several instances, helped found, many of the reform and social justice organizations labeled as "Red" in the spider-web charts, including WILPF, the National Child Labor Committee, and the American Civil Liberties Union (ACLU).

AN ENDURING LEGACY

Partly in response to the Red Scare, Addams spent much of the early 1920s abroad. In early 1923, she and her close friend, Mary Rozet Smith, embarked on a nine-month, round-the-world journey, which included stops in India, Japan, China, and the Philippines. "Wherever she went, the reception was warm; in some places, even triumphant," Addams's biographer Jean Bethke Elshtain writes.[5] Despite suffering a series of health crises during the 1920s, Addams also continued to oversee Hull House, lecture often on pacifism, and write books, including her second autobiographical volume, *The Second Twenty Years at Hull-House*, covering the period from 1909 to 1929.

By the time *The Second Twenty Years* was published in 1930, Addams's reputation in the United States had dramatically improved. During the Great Depression, which lasted from late 1929 through most of the 1930s, Addams's tireless efforts on behalf of the Nineteenth Ward's hungry and unemployed endeared her to the American press and public. Once again she was showered with awards and honors for her selfless devotion to social justice and humanitarian causes. In May 1931, Addams received the greatest honor of her life when she became the first American woman to be awarded the Nobel Peace Prize for her longtime commitment to pacifism. Characteristically, rather than keep the prize money—approximately $16,000—for herself, Addams promptly donated it to the Women's International League for Peace and Freedom.

In 1931, Jane Addams won the Nobel Peace Prize in recognition of her many years of pacifist activities. By the 1930s, Addams's reputation had improved, and her efforts on behalf of the Nineteenth Ward's residents during the Great Depression once again endeared her to the public.

Addams's health continued to decline during the early 1930s. In February 1934, while she was recovering from a serious bout of bronchitis, she was devastated by the death of her longtime friend and companion, Mary Rozet Smith, from pneumonia. Addams lived on for another 15 months after Smith, spending much of her time writing what was to be her last book: a memoir of Hull House resident and social reformer Julia Lathrop, who had died in 1932. On May 17, 1935, Addams was admitted to a Chicago hospital complaining of severe abdominal pain. The next day she underwent surgery for an intestinal tumor. Three days later, on May 21, 1935, Jane Addams died at age 74.

Expressions of sympathy flooded into Hull House from around the United States and the world. Addams's coffin was placed in the settlement house's auditorium, and thousands of mourners, many of them Nineteenth Ward neighbors, came to pay their final respects to America's most famous female humanitarian. On May 23, friends and family jammed into the settlement house courtyard for a nondenominational funeral service. Afterward, Addams's body was transported to her hometown of Cedarville and buried in a small cemetery near her parents, in accordance with her wishes.

By the end of the 1930s, the government-sponsored social welfare programs instituted as part of President Franklin D. Roosevelt's New Deal had started to supplant the thriving settlement movement Jane Addams had helped found in the United States. Nonetheless, Hull House continued to serve the Halsted Street community for nearly three decades after Addams's death. In 1963, most of the complex was demolished to make room for the Chicago campus of the University of Illinois. The original Hull mansion and one other building, the Residents' Dining Hall, are now a museum and educational center celebrating Addams's life and work as well as the contributions of her

Jane Addams toured Hull House in May 1935 with a group of young visitors. Later that month, on May 17, Addams was hospitalized with severe abdominal pain; four days later, she was dead at the age of 74.

dedicated Hull House colleagues, including Julia Lathrop, Alice Hamilton, and Florence Kelley.

Although Hull House ceased to function as a settlement house nearly five decades ago, Addams's humanitarian vision endures in the Jane Addams Hull House Association, Chicago's largest social and human service agency. Currently, the association operates four community centers in working-class neighborhoods in and around Chicago, offering educational programs, job training, senior and family services, small business development, and housing assistance to more than 60,000 men, women, and children each year. In keeping with Addams's own commitment to social justice reform, the association also champions a variety of public policy reforms aimed at removing barriers to economic self-sufficiency and improving living conditions for the poor, racial minorities, and other at-risk urban populations.

Today, Addams's humanitarian legacy lives on not only in the endeavors and vision of the Jane Addams Hull House Association but in the many enduring progressive social reforms and organizations with which she was associated, from child labor reform and women's suffrage to the NAACP and the ACLU. Her unswerving commitment to social, economic, and racial justice is also reflected in the Jane Addams College of Social Work of the University of Illinois at Chicago, whose self-stated purpose is to carry forward Addams's humanitarian mission, adapting it to the contemporary needs and realities of the inner city. Three-quarters of a century after her death, Addams's works and ideals continue to shape the social work profession she helped pioneer and inspire all those who seek to achieve greater meaning and purpose in their lives by striving to create a more just and humane society.

CHRONOLOGY

1860	Born in Cedarville, Illinois, on September 6.
1863	Mother, Sarah Weber Addams, dies.
1868	Father, John Addams, marries Anna Haldeman.
1877–1881	Attends Rockford Female Seminary.
1881	Father dies in August, leaving Jane with a substantial inheritance.
1882	Leaves medical school after one semester.
1888	Visits Toynbee Hall, a pioneering social settlement house in London.
1889	Cofounds Hull House with Ellen Gates Starr in Chicago's Nineteenth Ward.
1895	Is appointed garbage inspector for the Nineteenth Ward.
1905	Becomes a member of the Chicago Board of Education.
1909	Helps found the National Association for the Advancement of Colored People; is elected the first female president of the National Conference of Social Work.
1910	Addams's autobiography, *Twenty Years at Hull-House*, is published.
1911	Becomes vice president of the National American Woman Suffrage Association.
1912	Campaigns for Theodore Roosevelt, the Progressive Party candidate for president.
1915	Is elected the first chairwoman of the Women's Peace Party; attends the

International Peace Congress of Women at The Hague, Netherlands.

1919   Is elected the first president of the Women's International League for Peace and Freedom.

1920   Helps found the American Civil Liberties Union.

1931   Is awarded the Nobel Peace Prize.

1935   Dies in Chicago on May 21 at age 74.

NOTES

CHAPTER 1

1. Jane Addams, *Twenty Years at Hull-House*. New York: Macmillan, 1910, p. 198.
2. Quoted in Allen F. Davis, *American Heroine: The Life and Legend of Jane Addams*. Chicago: Ivan R. Dee, 1973, p. 291.

CHAPTER 2

1. Quoted in James Weber Linn, *Jane Addams: A Biography*. 1935. Reprint. Urbana: University of Illinois Press, 2000, p. 22.
2. Addams, *Twenty Years at Hull-House*, pp. 1; 11.
3. Ibid., p. 11.
4. Ibid., pp. 7; 9.
5. Quoted in Louise W. Knight, *Citizen: Jane Addams and the Struggle for Democracy*. Chicago: University of Chicago Press, 2005, p. 27.
6. Addams, *Twenty Years at Hull-House*, pp. 2–3.
7. Gioia Diliberto, *A Useful Woman: The Early Life of Jane Addams*. New York: Scribner, 1999, p. 52.
8. Addams, *Twenty Years at Hull-House*, pp. 3; 5.
9. Ibid., p. 5.
10. Diliberto, *A Useful Woman*, p. 48.
11. Davis, *American Heroine*, p. 7.
12. Knight, *Citizen*, p. 48.
13. Linn, *Jane Addams*, p. 34.
14. Barbara Garland Polikoff, *With One Bold Act: The Story of Jane Addams*. Chicago: Boswell Books, 1999, p. 12.

CHAPTER 3

1. Quoted in Knight, *Citizen*, p. 64.
2. Addams, *Twenty Years at Hull-House*, p. 43.
3. Davis, *American Heroine*, p. 10.

4. Quoted in Linn, *Jane Addams*, p. 411; p. 40.

5. Diliberto, *A Useful Woman*, p. 56.

6. Quoted in Davis, *American Heroine*, p. 6.

7. Quoted in Polikoff, *With One Bold Act*, p. 28.

8. Quoted in Davis, *American Heroine*, p. 11.

9. Knight, *Citizen*, p. 81.

10. Addams, *Twenty Years at Hull-House*, p. 56.

11. Quoted in Polikoff, *With One Bold Act*, pp. 23–24.

12. Quoted in Davis, *American Heroine*, p. 12.

13. Quoted in Linn, *Jane Addams*, p. 47.

14. Knight, *Citizen*, p. 94.

15. Victoria Bissell Brown, *The Education of Jane Addams*. Philadelphia: University of Pennsylvania Press, 2004, p. 66.

CHAPTER 4

1. Quoted in Knight, *Citizen*, p. 107.

2. Davis, *American Heroine*, p. 9.

3. Quoted in Diliberto, *A Useful Woman*, p. 83.

4. Quoted in Polikoff, *With One Bold Act*, p. 35.

5. Quoted in Knight, *Citizen*, p. 115.

6. Diliberto, *A Useful Woman*, p. 85.

7. Quoted in Diliberto, *A Useful Woman*, p. 85.

8. Quoted in Polikoff, *With One Bold Act*, pp. 36–37.

9. Davis, *American Heroine*, p. 29.

10. Diliberto, *A Useful Woman*, p. 94.

11. Davis, *American Heroine*, p. 32.

12. Addams, *Twenty Years at Hull-House*, p. 68.

13. Ibid., p. 74.

14. Quoted in Polikoff, *With One Bold Act*, p. 45.

15. Quoted in Diliberto, *A Useful Woman*, p. 104.

16. Ibid., pp. 118–119.

17. Addams, *Twenty Years at Hull-House*, p. 86.

18. Ibid., pp. 85; 87.

CHAPTER 5

1. Quoted in Davis, *American Heroine*, p. 49.
2. Diliberto, *A Useful Woman*, p. 145.
3. Quoted in Polikoff, *With One Bold Act*, pp. 60–61.
4. Davis, *American Heroine*, p. 55.
5. Quoted in Davis, *American Heroine*, p. 57.
6. Knight, *Citizen*, p. 195.
7. Addams, *Twenty Years at Hull-House*, pp. 97–100.
8. Polikoff, *With One Bold Act*, p. 65.
9. Diliberto, *A Useful Woman*, p. 158.
10. Linn, *Jane Addams*, p. 115.
11. Quoted in Davis, *American Heroine*, p. 81.
12. Quoted in Polikoff, *With One Bold Act*, p. 72.
13. Quoted in Jean Bethke Elshtain, *Jane Addams and the Dream of American Democracy*. New York: Basic Books, 2001, p. 11.
14. Addams, *Twenty Years at Hull-House*, p. 110.
15. Linn, *Jane Addams*, p. 113.
16. Davis, *American Heroine*, p. 78.

CHAPTER 6

1. Addams, *Twenty Years at Hull-House*, pp. 198–199.
2. Quoted in Diliberto, *A Useful Woman*, p. 198.
3. Knight, *Citizen*, p. 213.
4. Quoted in Polikoff, *With One Bold Act*, p. 102.
5. Davis, *American Heroine*, pp. 110–111.
6. Quoted in Davis, *American Heroine*, p. 114.
7. Addams, *Twenty Years at Hull-House*, p. 283.
8. Diliberto, *A Useful Woman*, p. 217.
9. Quoted in Diliberto, *A Useful Woman*, p. 217.
10. Quoted in Elshtain, *Jane Addams*, p. 186.
11. Quoted in Polikoff, *With One Bold Act*, p. 146.
12. Diliberto, *A Useful Woman*, pp. 237–238.
13. Davis, *American Heroine*, p. 201.

CHAPTER 7

1. Jane Addams, *The Second Twenty Years at Hull-House, September 1909 to September 1929, with a Record of a Growing World Consciousness*. New York: Macmillan, 1930, p. 33.
2. Quoted in Davis, *American Heroine*, p. 194.
3. Ibid., p. 192.
4. Davis, *American Heroine*, p. 197.
5. Quoted in Polikoff, *With One Bold Act*, p. 175.
6. Quoted in Linn, *Jane Addams*, p. 314.
7. Quoted in Diliberto, *A Useful Woman*, p. 261.
8. Davis, *American Heroine*, p. 226.
9. Polikoff, *With One Bold Act*, p. 182.

CHAPTER 8

1. Quoted in Linn, *Jane Addams*, p. 345.
2. Ibid., pp. 348–349.
3. Quoted in Davis, *American Heroine*, p. 267.
4. Ibid., p. 264.
5. Elshtain, *Jane Addams*, p. 245.

BIBLIOGRAPHY

Addams, Jane. *The Second Twenty Years at Hull-House, September 1909 to September 1929, with a Record of a Growing World Consciousness*. New York: Macmillan, 1930.

———. *Twenty Years at Hull-House*. New York: Macmillan, 1910.

Brown, Victoria Bissell. *The Education of Jane Addams*. Philadelphia: University of Pennsylvania Press, 2004.

Davis, Allen F. *American Heroine: The Life and Legend of Jane Addams*. Chicago: Ivan R. Dee, 1973.

Diliberto, Gioia. *A Useful Woman: The Early Life of Jane Addams*. New York: Scribner, 1999.

Elshtain, Jean Bethke. *Jane Addams and the Dream of American Democracy*. New York: Basic Books, 2001.

Johnson, Gordon. "Hull House Shows How to Solve Ills." *Chicago Tribune*, September 8, 1992.

Knight, Louise W. *Citizen: Jane Addams and the Struggle for Democracy*. Chicago: University of Chicago Press, 2005.

Linn, James Weber. *Jane Addams: A Biography*. 1935. Reprint. Urbana: University of Illinois Press, 2000.

Pacyga, Dominic A. *Chicago: A Biography*. Chicago: University of Chicago Press, 2009.

Polikoff, Barbara Garland. *With One Bold Act: The Story of Jane Addams*. Chicago: Boswell Books, 1999.

FURTHER RESOURCES

BOOKS

Caravantes, Peggy. *Waging Peace: The Story of Jane Addams.* Greensboro, N.C.: Morgan Reynolds, 2004.

Fradin, Judith Bloom, and Dennis Brindell Fradin. *Jane Addams: Champion of Democracy.* New York: Clarion Books, 2006.

Harvey, Bonnie Carman. *Jane Addams: Nobel Prize Winner and Founder of Hull House.* Berkeley Heights, N.J.: Enslow Publishers, 1999.

Johnson, Mary Ann, ed. *The Many Faces of Hull-House: The Photographs of Wallace Kirkland.* Urbana: University of Illinois Press, 1989.

Knight, Louise W. *Jane Addams: Spirit in Action.* New York: W.W. Norton & Company, 2010.

WEB SITES

Chicago, City of the Century: Jane Addams
http://www.pbs.org/wgbh/amex/chicago/peopleevents/p_addams.html

Jane Addams: Hull-House Museum
http://www.uic.edu/jaddams/hull/hull_house.html

Jane Addams: The Nobel Peace Prize 1931
http://nobelprize.org/nobel_prizes/peace/laureates/1931/addams-bio.html

The Jane Addams Papers Project
http://www.janeaddamsproject.org

Urban Experience in Chicago: Hull-House and Its Neighborhoods, 1889–1963
http://www.uic.edu/jaddams/hull/urbanexp/contents.htm

PICTURE CREDITS

INDEX

ABOUT THE AUTHOR

LOUISE CHIPLEY SLAVICEK received her master's degree in American history from the University of Connecticut. She is the author of numerous articles on American and world history for scholarly journals and young people's magazines, including *Cobblestone, Calliope,* and *Highlights for Children.* Her more than two-dozen books for young people include *Women of the American Revolution, I.M. Pei,* and *The Chinese Cultural Revolution.*